ITALIANS IN THE LOWCOUNTRY

"Sunny Italy's Charleston Colony"

BY CHRISTINA R. BUTLER

For

Dante Alighieri Society of Charleston

Copyright © 2021 Dante Alighieri Society of Charleston

ISBN: 9780578884028

Interior Design Layout By Tami Boyce
www.tamiboyce.com

Front Cover:

Villa Margherita is a 9,000 square foot villa at 4 South Battery. Andrew Simonds, founder and president of the First National Bank of South Carolina, built the house as a gift to his flamboyant wife Daisy in 1895. Inspired by a previous trip to Italy, Simonds commissioned the renowned architect Frederick P. Dinkelberg, who also designed Manhattan's famous Flatiron building, to design the house, merging currently popular Beaux Arts features with the Renaissance Revival style seen in Italy. "Daisy" (margherita in Italian) Beaux Simonds, a beautiful socialite from New Orleans, personally painted clouds with roses on the drawing room ceiling.

Italian influence can be seen in the fluted Corinthian columns over the front entrance, a cast-iron Florentine balcony, and a fireplace adorned with plaster cherubs and caryatids.

Back cover:

"Multiple illustrations of phosphate mining, Charleston, South Carolina" from *Leslie's Illustrated Magazine* shows laborers at work in Lowcountry mills and mines in the late nineteenth century. Hundreds of newly arrived Italians toiled in the industry, and mine owners even actively recruited new immigrants from New York to relocate to Charleston for work. Italian miners were often exploited, and Consul Giovanni Sottile took their plight to the South Carolina district attorney to fight for their rights.

Dante Alighieri Society of Charleston

The Dante Alighieri Society of Charleston commissioned this history of Italians in Charleston to celebrate the 700th anniversary of the death of Dante Alighieri, the Florentine poet revered as the "father" of the Italian language.

The Dante Alighieri Society of Charleston is a non-profit organization affiliated with the international Società Dante Alighieri, founded in 1889 to promote Italian culture and language around the world. The Charleston chapter sponsors public events to share Italian culture and history with residents of the Low Country. It offers Italian language lessons, supports the annual Nuovo Cinema Italiano Film Festival, and is proud to be associated with the Ashley Hall School.

TABLE OF CONTENTS

Forward		vii
Introduction		ix
Chapter 1	Italians in the Colonial Era	1
Chapter 2	The Federal Era	5
Chapter 3	The Antebellum Era	11
Chapter 4	Increased Italian Immigration in Postbellum Charleston	17
Chapter 5	Important Italian Families at the turn of the century	23
Chapter 6	Italians in the City of Charleston in the early Twentieth Century	39
Chapter 7	World War II to the late Twentieth Century	45
Chapter 8	Spoleto Festival U.S.A.	51
Chapter 9	Italian Americans in Twenty First Century Charleston	61
Chapter 10	Italians in Charleston Today	67
Conclusion		81
Bibliography		83
Appendix 1: Transcription from Motes, Margaret Peckham. Migration to South Carolina- 1850 Census.		89

FORWARD

Italians in the Lowcountry is a fascinating journey through the origins of Italian immigration to Charleston and South Carolina. It explores, deeply, the roots of a group of diverse and pioneering Italian travelers who decided to settle and prosper in the Southeast of the United States.

It graciously rediscovers and reconnects this ancient heritage to those who, only recently arriving from Italy, made Charleston their new home. Our compatriots' stories – starting from silk merchants, grocery shop owners, and farmers to artists, researchers, and architects – have all shaped the city's atmosphere. They are an example of how Italians contributed and continue to contribute to the social and economic development of the United States, and namely of the community in the South-East.

The tales of hope, integration, success, and failure described in this book are those of many Italian migrants I have witnessed in the world and a reaffirmation of our culture's very nature. Talent, creativity, an open mindset, innovation, perseverance, and resilience are the fundamental traits that make Italians abroad vibrant and attractive.

Our innate yearning to connect with each other and our nation creates the perfect blend for bridging cultures and traditions, bringing together the past and the present to lay the foundation of future achievements.

I am deeply thankful to Christina R. Butler and to the Dante Alighieri Society for having unveiled Italians' journey in Charleston and for the value that her work signifies to the growing residents of Italian origins in the area and the whole local community.

Cristiano Musillo
Consul General of Italy in Miami

INTRODUCTION

Charleston, South Carolina is a 350-year-old port city, and like any community with a maritime heritage, it has a rich history full of diverse residents. It is home to the oldest Italian American community in the Southeast. The city never attracted immigrants in large numbers, as there was labor competition from the majority enslaved African and African American population before the American Civil War. Anti-Catholic sentiment in the colonial era left most potential immigrants from Spain, France, and Italy unwelcome. In the late nineteenth century, the city's economy stagnated and further precluded a mass infusion of European immigrants. Still, as a maritime city, Charleston had a contingent of Italians in its early days, and in the late nineteenth and early twentieth century, the city was home to a small but important and diverse minority of Italians who worked hard in their chosen new city and operated integral businesses. Some toiled in phosphate mines and on farms in Charleston County. In the city, they worked as tradesmen and laborers, and operated successful restaurants, taverns, wholesale groceries, and fruit shops. A lucky few, like the Sottile and Chicco families, rose to the upper echelons of Charleston society in the quintessential American dream. In the twenty-first century, recently arrived Italians continue to enhance the city's cultural and artistic life, and Italian American Charlestonians remain an important and proud community descended from hardworking immigrants. This book seeks to add the often overlooked but important and diverse stories, biographies, and experiences of Charleston's Italians and Italian Americans to the city's historical narrative. It is but a first step in documenting Italians in the Lowcountry and will hopefully inspire others to explore their family's roots and to discover the stories of the thousands of Italians that helped make the city what it is today. This work was graciously sponsored by the Dante Alighieri Society, Charleston Chapter, with special thanks to Donatella Cappelletti and Bob Gebhardt, without whom this book would not have been possible.

CHAPTER 1:

ITALIANS IN THE COLONIAL ERA

As the capital town of an English colony (first proprietary and then royal), Charlestown enticed few Italians in the seventeenth and eighteenth century. Italy at that time was composed of various kingdoms or principalities (Sardinia, Sicily, Venice, Duchy of Milan, the Papal States in Rome, among others.) The kingdoms were not unified and were subject to periodic invasion by the French and Spanish, and Italy experienced internal struggles as the regions and kingdoms fought to solidify their borders.

The French and Spanish were often at war with England, and by extension her colonies, precluding Italians from being able to emigrate to South Carolina. Virtually all of the Italian kingdoms and duchies were majority Catholic, further reducing the appeal of the majority-Protestant English colonies as a destination for emigration. Lastly, Italy had yet to experience a large outward migration, so relatively few citizens were journeying to the new American colonies.

Italian Architectural and Cultural Influence in Early South Carolina

There was a market for Italian culture and products in Charlestown, however, and merchants imported Italian linens, silks, marble tabletops, silk flowers for millinery and dressmaking, and Italian-made riding chairs. Merchants regularly advertised these products for sale, "just imported", in their King Street and East Bay Street shops.

Italian Renaissance architecture influenced English design in both the United Kingdom and her American colonies in the seventeenth and eighteenth centuries. Andrea Palladio (1508-1580) was one of the most influential architects of the Renaissance, known both for his functional and beautiful villa designs and for publishing a treatise on the Roman writer Vitruvius' works. The son of a stone carver, he was a practical designer but also had a deep interest in classical features and proportions. Palladio analyzed the ruins in Rome and studied Raphael, Michelangelo, and Giulio Romano (a founder of the Mannerist movement). He published *The Four Books of Architecture* which became wildly popular in English translation about one hundred years after his death. The

Neo Palladians, a group of English-speaking architects and master builders in England and colonies including South Carolina, sought to incorporate the great Paduan master's design principles into their English villa designs. Charlestown bookshops offered for sale the latest translations of Alberti's and Palladio's architectural pattern books.

Several of Charleston's elites had titles in their private libraries displaying their knowledge and interest in Italian Renaissance architects and owned books on the ancient Classics, as well as English Renaissance architectural treatises of the Neo Palladians. Joseph Manigault's 1771 inventory, for example, included William Pain's English translation of Palladio's *Four Books of Architecture, Lives of the First Roman Emperors,* and a Latin copy of *Virgil*. Similarly, the Charleston Library Society has important Italian titles in their collection that date from its early collections and speak further to Charlestonians' interests in the latest cultural and artistic works coming out of Italy: Piranesi's *Colonna Antonina* plates of Marcus Aurelius' memorial columns (1776) and *Vasi, candelabra, cippi, sarcophagi, tripod, Lucerne ed ornamenti antichi disegn* (1778).

Drayton Hall, established in 1738, is the earliest example of high-style Palladian architecture in South Carolina, and as its *South Carolina Encyclopedia* entry notes, "at the time of its construction, its two-story, brick main house with raised basement was representative of current English Georgian architecture and was inspired by the designs of the Italian Renaissance architect Andrea Palladio. However, its recessed, two-story portico – the earliest of its kind in America – probably had no English precedent and was directly derived from Palladio's *The Four Books of Architecture*, republished in 1715. Thus, Drayton Hall combined Old World design and eighteenth-century fashion with the tastes of the owner, the abilities of colonial craftspeople – black and white, free and enslaved – and the climate of the Lowcountry to create a uniquely American architectural form." John Drayton, the amateur architect and owner of Drayton Hall, had Palladio's *Four Books* in his personal collection, as well as *Vitruvius Britannicus* (Colin Campbell, 1715), *Palladio Londinensus* (William Salmon, 1734), and Neo-Palladian James Gibbes' *Book of Architecture* (1728). As Drayton Hall curator Trish Lowe Smith notes, "during this time [1715-1748] British Palladian architecture became the predominant style", as Renaissance architectural ideas took root in the Atlantic colonial world. Drayton Hall draws features from Villa Cornaro near Venice (designed by Palladio in 1551) and is noteworthy for its early use in the United States of a projecting double story portico. The floor plan also utilizes Palladio's preferred ratios and modules of interior layout.

Drayton Hall, a quintessential early South Carolina example of Georgian Palladian architecture, constructed circa 1740.

ITALIANS IN THE COLONIAL ERA

In the city, the Miles Brewton House completed circa 1769 is by far the best example of Georgian Palladian architectural ideals, modeled partly on Palladio's Villa Pisani, but like Drayton Hall, it is a fusion of several plates and designs to create a unique local commission. The exterior is noteworthy for its two-story pedimented porch, with Doric columns on the first story and Ionic on the second. Josiah Quincy described the house when he visited in 1773 as having "the grandest hall I ever beheld."

Many of the first Italians to arrive in Charleston had artistic backgrounds or were skilled in trades. They arrived by way of France or London from the northern areas of Italy, while later waves of Italian immigrants were more often from an agricultural background and emigrating from the southern regions and Sicily. A Mr. Lewis Vidal, for example, possibly of Italian extraction, arrived in Charleston in 1774 and advertised to teach ladies and gentlemen to sing and play Italian instruments. He had previously performed in the courts of Portugal. Vidal noted that he knew little English but could be hired to teach French and Italian language. Benjamin Goy was also taking students in French and Italian in the 1770s, as was Andrew Siri at his house on Church Street (Siri had arrived by way of England, and also offered instruction in the "Italian method of book-keeping.") Perhaps the most unique reference to Italian speakers was an advertisement for an enslaved man brought to the Workhouse in June 1759: "A tall black Negro fellow Angola born, says name is Larry, and belongs to Mr. Bonneau at Santee, has on an old blue jacket with powder buttons and a pair of old white negro cloth breeches, he had his left arm broke by a blow from some white person, and by what can be discovered in his speech, is either Spanish or Italian."

Siri's advertisement to teach Italian, *South Carolina Gazette,* 12 June 1764.

The Amatis Family and Piedmont Italians in Purrysburg, South Carolina.

Colonists in early South Carolina experimented with a variety of potential cash crops suited to the subtropical climate, which led to a short-lived but intense interest in growing mulberry trees to cultivate silk. Paolo and Nicola Amatis, who came from a family of silk merchants in Turin, were among the first settlers to Georgia. Paolo was recorded in the original "List of the persons sent to Georgia on the charity of the trustees for establishing the colony there", and his entry noted, he "understands the nature & production of raw silk." By 1733 Paolo was in Charleston planting and tending orange and mulberry trees and a grape vineyard on the South side of Broad Street, near today's Orange Street. The Amatis brothers also brought several Italians as servants who were also from the Piedmont region of Italy (surrounding Turin and bordered by France and Switzerland.) Additionally, around forty more Italian Protestants arrived through Charleston and settled in Purrysburg, a vibrant but now defunct town in today's Jasper County, South Carolina, to work with the silk experiments. Historian Ben Marsh notes that, "on either side of the Savannah River [Georgia and Jasper County, South Carolina] the French and Swiss settlers, German speakers from various principalities, and Piedmontese Italians who clustered in and around these townships made the most substantial contribution to silk production of any group in the lower South." Most of the trees were then transplanted to Savannah in 1735, although Paolo remained in Charleston until his death in December 1736.

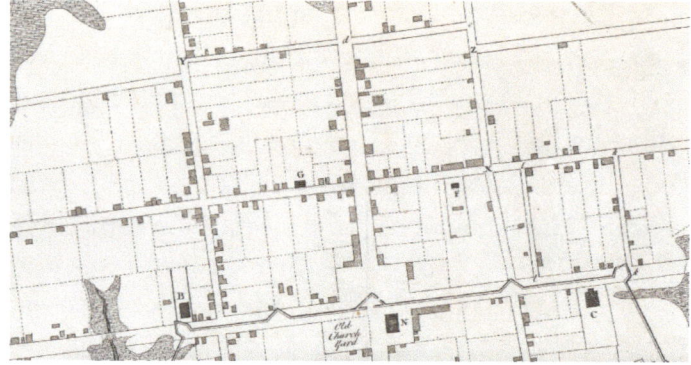

Charlestown on a 1739 map, showing the vestiges of the town wall and "Old church yard" (the original site of St. Philip's Church) at Meeting and Broad Street, and the former site of the Orange Garden (block Y-D-G.)

A map of South Carolina from the Savannah Sound to St. Helena's Sound, by Brailsford and Hodgson, showing Jasper County and Purrysburg. 1771. Library of Congress.

Anti-Catholic Sentiments in the Colonial Era

As an English colony in which English laws applied and Anglicanism was the majority (and state backed) religion, Catholics were viewed with suspicion, and essentially banned entirely, from colonial South Carolina. This doubtless curtailed any interest that most Italian immigrants might have had in coming into Charleston, although several did arrive as mariners and sailors, and a few stayed in the colony. Historian Dr. Nic Butler explained that the Penal Laws enacted in England and in force in parts of the British Empire into the nineteenth century were instated to strip the civil liberties of Catholics who remained faithful to the Church of Rome. The Fundamental Constitutions of Carolina, adopted by the Lords Proprietors who founded the colony, allowed for the collection of taxes "to be employed in the exercise of religion, according to the Church of England, which being the only true and orthodox and the national religion of all the King's dominions, is so also of Carolina." Catholics were not included in the Toleration Act of 1689 which allowed non-Anglican Protestants to worship in Carolina. Further fueling religious paranoia was the fact that for much of the colonial era, England was at war with France and Spain, both majority Catholic countries with colonial holdings near South Carolina, which caused the English to be especially wary of foreigners who might have allegiances to enemy countries as well as to the "Papist" faith.

CHAPTER 2:

THE FEDERAL ERA

Anti-Catholic sentiment, and with it, distrust of the Spanish and Italians, began to fade in the early Republic. There were still relatively few Italians in Charleston, however, both because the Kingdoms and principalities of Italy had yet to see a large-scale outmigration, and because there were few job opportunities to entice immigrants to the American South.

The *South Carolina Gazette and Daily Advertiser* reprinted a description in December, 1783 by a Revd. Sherlock for a Charleston audience, should they ever travel to Italy or encounter a recent immigrant, which offers a window into the continued prejudice against Catholics and stereotypes directed at Italians in the late eighteenth century: "mediocrity is rare here [Italy]; everything is in extremes. . . an excessive luxury amongst individuals, and people in the most abject misery . . . it is the same in regard to religion, you will see nothing but a blind superstition or determined atheists. The Italian in general is exceedingly good, or wicket to a degree. Men are born here with strong passions, and not receiving an education, it is not astonishing that they commit great crimes. Love, jealous, and revenge are their ruling passion . . . they have ungoverned imaginations and no philosophy. And why has good taste not penetrated Italy? Because Italy has neither a London nor a Paris; and she has never had a Louis the fourteenth. Travelers are often mistaken in judging of the Italian, especially the Neapolitan. They think he has no sense, because he wants ideas. . . he resembles the soil of his own country; a field well tilled in Naples produces the most plentiful crops; neglected it yields but briars and thistles. It is the same with the genius of the inhabitants; cultivated, it is capable of everything; untilled, it produces only folly and vice."

Founding the Catholic Church in South Carolina

Following the American Revolution, religious freedom became a protected right in the United States, and Catholics in South Carolina began worshiping publicly and freely. According to St. Mary's Greenville, "the recorded history of Catholics in South Carolina begins in 1786 when an Italian priest who was a passenger on a ship that was called at Charleston Harbor celebrated Mass in a private home for twelve people." The new State of South Carolina revised its constitution to finally allow true religious freedom, stating, "the free exercise and enjoyment of religious profession and worship, without discrimination or preference, shall forever hereafter be allowed within this state to all mankind." In 1789, St. Mary's Church, the first Roman Catholic congregation in South Carolina, was founded, and it was incorporated by the South Carolina legislature in 1791. Catholics were still a small minority in Charleston (the largest city in the state in the federal era), and the first priest, Matthew Ryan, noted that the roughly 200 Catholics in his congregation were "few, poor, and timid."

St. Mary's congregation grew with an influx of French refugees from St. Domingue (now Haiti) who were fleeing a slave insurrection and revolution in the 1790s. As more Irish arrived in Charleston in the coming decades, several new churches were formed (St. Patrick's and the Cathedral of St. Finbar on Broad Street) and St. Mary's became predominantly French. In the antebellum era there were not enough Italians in the city to create their own ethnic Catholic congregation. There are several Italians buried in St. Mary's small graveyard adjacent to the Hasell Street building, with headstones dating to the late eighteenth and early nineteenth century, indicating that they were among the founding members.

The current church building on Hasell Street replaced an earlier building that burned in the Fire of 1838. It is in the Classical Revival style made popular in South Carolina by the architect Robert Mills, although he did not design the church. The ceiling was executed by the decorative painter Chizzola, while the walls feature over twenty additional paintings by Cesare Portia, an Italian artist, which were installed in 1896.

St. Mary's of the Annunciation, Hasell Street.

The Catholic churches, St. Mary's included, began running out of burial space, so St. Lawrence Catholic Cemetery, with its intricate wrought and cast-iron cross monument at the entrance, was opened in 1854. Many of Charleston's Italian and Italian American residents were buried there and the cemetery remains active today.

THE FEDERAL ERA

St. Lawrence Catholic Cemetery, established 1851.

Noteworthy Italians in the early nineteenth century

Italians in federal era Charleston were often musically inclined and culturally sophisticated and were likely attracted to the city because of its cosmopolitan reputation. Augustino Fromento advertised in January 1808 that he was "lately [arrived] from Italy" and had established a shop on Broad Street where "he cuts and dresses hair in the neatest style and in a particular manner, so as to adapt it to the physiognomy and shape of the head. The experience which he has had from the practice of his trade in various cities noted for taste and elegance, induces him to flatter himself, that his mode of dressing the hair will give universal satisfaction." He also had lavender water and various perfumes, soaps, and combs offered for sale.

Geatano Franceschini, a violinist and composer, arrived in Charleston by 1774, and performed several concerts for the St. Cecelia Society, the first concert patronage society in colonial America. After leaving South Carolina in 1775, he returned in 1780 to offer concerts after the British capture of the city during the American Revolution, before departing permanently for New York in 1782.

Philip Trajetta (born 1777 in Naples as Filippo Trajetta- died 1854) was the son of a famous opera composer. He studied music in Venice and Paris (where he was imprisoned in 1798 for involvement in Revolutionary activities before he escaped) and then moved to Boston in 1799. Trajetta came to Charleston in 1801 where he was active in local musical life before becoming involved in a feud over a new opera in 1810. He then moved to New York and later Philadelphia, where he established the American Conservatorio in 1823. Teresa Mazzulli of the *Boston Intelligencer* states that, "Trajetta's sojourn of about eight years in Charleston proved to be a time of great creativity and professional accomplishments for the newly arrived immigrant musician. There he found a welcoming city with a rich history of early music appreciation. The St. Cecilia Society of Charleston, known as the oldest musical institution in North America, which was formed by a group of gentlemen amateur musicians who enjoyed gathering together and playing in the orchestral ensemble, invited professional musicians for the city for an annual concert season. Trajetta was a skilled violinist with impeccable Old World musical credentials, and was possibly a fellow of the St. Cecilia Society. Trajetta was soon known in Charleston as a professor of music, vocal and instrumental performer, composer, conductor and poet. His *Sinfonia Concertata*, composed in 1803 and performed at St. Cecilia Concert Room on February 26, 1805, was said to be the best symphonic work composed on American soil near the beginning of the 19th century. The hypothesis that Filippo Trajetta's *Tre Quartetti Concertati* are works he also composed while in Charleston would attribute these compositions by him as the first of that genre composed on American soil."

Trajetta's ad in the *Charleston City Gazette*, 29 January 1802.

Charlestonians Abroad on early Grand Tours: John Izard Middleton and Joseph Allen Smith

Like the English aristocracy they sought to emulate, late eighteenth-century Charlestonians traveled to the Continent to explore European art and architecture, especially the ancient Classics and the Renaissance masters. Mary Stead Pinckney remarked of her trip abroad, "how can any written account convey to you an idea - the grade and beauty of the heads of Guido [Mazzoni, an early 16th century Italian sculptor]?" Ralph and Alice DeLancey Izard made a trip to Herculaneum and Pompei in 1775, becoming some of the first Americans to see the newly excavated Roman ruins there. Mrs. Izard wrote, "we have received great pleasure from our tour- I have met with nothing that seems so extraordinary to me as the neighborhood of this place, the beautiful pieces of antiquity, that have been found in them, surpasses all imagination." They continued southward to the Greek ruins of Paestum in Salerno, Italy in their pursuit of classical antiquity.

John Izard Middleton (1785-1849) was an intriguing South Carolinian, born to Mary Izard and Arthur Middleton and raised at Middleton Place before finding a passion for studying abroad. He studied at Cambridge and was accepted by the highest cosmopolitan social circles in Europe, which unlocked important travel opportunities for him. Middleton arrived in Italy in 1807 and stayed for several years, studying the great writers and buildings from classical antiquity. He began to draw the ruins and compiled archeological notes which were printed in 1812. Middleton married the daughter of a Neapolitan banker and spent the remainder of his life in Europe, dying in Paris in 1849. Maurie McInnis writes that Middleton's "architectural designs demonstrate the combination of local vernacular traditions and an extensive knowledge of European design to considerable advantage.' He was "a true figure of the Enlightenment . . . well acquainted with the leading European intellectuals, and his own interests in classical antiquity led to the 1812 publication, *Grecian Remains in Italy*."

Joseph Allen Smith (1769-1828) was born to the prestigious Smith family in South Carolina, and like Middleton, spent several years abroad on a Grand Tour to Ireland, England, France, and Italy. According to Maurie McInnis, "Smith was associated with some of the leading intellectuals, artists, collectors, antiquarians, and dealers in Europe and he assembled an incomparable private collection. This notion was likely nurtured by his association in Italy with William Hamilton, British plenipotentiary to Naples, who was a dealer and collector of antiquities." Smith spent three years in Rome (1793-1796, during which he commissioned a portrait of his wife by Copley) and also traveled to Florence, where he visited the Tribuna. While in Italy, he purchased numerous pieces of artwork, including copies of the masters and new commissions, which his Italian agent John B. Sartori arranged to have sent back to the United States to create an extensive collection in Philadelphia. A contemporary named John Vaughn described the pieces in 1800 as "part of a collection which when in Italy Mr. Smith formed under the Idea, of collecting accurate presentations as he possibly could of those objects which were most admired." Smith purchased landscapes by 17th century master Salvator Rosa and by Guido Reni, Bartelemeo Schidone, and Andrea Lucatelli. His pieces became the foundation of the Pennsylvania Academy of Fine Arts in 1805, although only some of the thirteen crates Smith sent to the state made it, due to the Napoleonic Wars raging in Europe.

CHAPTER 3:

THE ANTEBELLUM ERA

Charleston's Italian population was small in the early nineteenth century. Most immigrants to the United States tended to flock to the North, where the cities were larger and factory work abounded. Only three Italian ships docked in Charleston between 1837 and 1848 (coming in from Sardinia and Genoa.)

The 1850 federal census (the first to list all members in each household) recorded at least 52 Italian-born residents in Charleston. There were nine females, none of whom were employed, as most were the wives or dependents of others. The men were employed as "fruiterers" (fruit sellers, 9 in total), mariners or fishermen (12), musicians (1), confectioners (1), statuary moulders (1), a laborer living in the poor house, a prisoner, cutlers (2), sawmill workers (1, aged 70), merchants, clerks, or shop keepers (10), painters (1), physicians (1), and tavern operators (1). Some of these residents were located in later census documents and city death records, while other Italians listed in 1850 either moved away or had their names so misspelled in later documents that they could not be relocated.

The *City of Charleston Census of 1861* listed only forty-five Italian born male residents in the city, twenty-six of whom were living in Ward 3 (Ansonborough.) There were only fourteen Italian born women, nine of whom were in Ansonborough.

A table showing Italian female population, by ward, from the 1861 *Census of the City of Charleston.*

Small Italian enclaves come to light by analyzing the 1861 *City Census* and later records. For example, several Italian-born residents lived on Market

Street. Andrew Drago resided next to Nicholas Tagierani. Angelo Canale lived at 13 Market Street in a building he owned, and his next-door neighbor was owner-occupant Angelo Bianci. Canale (1818-1897) was a merchant who had been living in Charleston for sixty years at the time of his death at 35 Society Street but was not recorded in the 1850 census. Moulder Nicholas Augustine lived nearby at Number 1 North Market. Louis Boniface (spelled myriad ways) lived a block to the north on Guignard Street in 1861. At the time of his death in 1891 at age 77, he was sadly destitute and living at the Alms House.

A small contingent of Italian immigrants lived on upper King Street in the mid to late nineteenth century. Fruit dealer and native of the Piedmont region Antonio Moroso was owner-occupant of 343 King Street. The Salvo brothers (James and Vincent) lived in houses they owned on upper King several blocks to the north. Their other brother Francis Salvo (born in 1792) owned and resided at 28 Vanderhorst Street and lived with his son James Salvo (age 19 and born in South Carolina, indicating that his father had emigrated to Charleston by 1830). The 1850 census also lists several members of the Gambale family in the Salvo household. A. Gambale was an Italian born merchant, living with his wife Agata. Also listed was Corado Salvo, a 63-year-old musician.

Italian Architecture in Antebellum Charleston

Though there are no known Italian born architects practicing in nineteenth century Charleston, there was no shortage of stylistic movements in that era that borrowed from Italian architectural themes. Master architects including South Carolina native Robert Mills continued to study the ancient Classics and Roman ruins in particular, to create classically proportioned and academically correct American architectural masterpieces of the new Greek Revival and Roman Revival movements. For example, Mills' Fireproof Building on Meeting Street features a Roman Doric portico and arched window openings. "The style of the plans generally was from the chastest models of Grecian and Roman architecture . . . from the remains of those most beautiful and venerable relics, which once adorned the magnificent temples of Attica and Italy," a contemporary said of Mills' buildings.

The Italianate style gained national popularity in the mid nineteenth century after appearing in Andrew Jackson Downing's *Architecture of Country Houses,* which featured suburban and rural house designs. Italianate houses were not modeled on true Italian Renaissance villas, but drew design references from them, articulated on a smaller scale, with less ornament, and usually constructed of brick or wood in the United States. Typical features included symmetrical overall design compositions, asymmetrical towers, blocky palazzo building forms (more popular for government and commercial examples than residential), arched window and door openings, wide cornices with brackets, cast iron decorative elements, and tall Italian windows two panes in width. One of the best Charleston examples is the John Ashe Jr. house at 26 South Battery, a Downing-esque design of stuccoed brick with arcaded porches and Italianate corbel brackets below the eaves, and the

THE ANTEBELLUM ERA

Patrick O'Donnell House, begun in 1852 at 21 King Street. The massive side hall house features an arched entry door, rusticated quoins, and arched window cornices. Roman Revival buildings, which often featured Roman temple porticos and intricate Composite order capitals, were also popular. The Jenkins Mikell House, constructed in 1853 on the corner of Rutledge and Montague Streets, exhibits these features.

The Patrick O'Donnell House on King Street and the Jenkins Mikell House at Montagu Street and Rutledge Avenue exemplify Italian Renaissance architectural influence in the city. Library of Congress.

The Italian Renaissance Revival movement of the later nineteenth century ushered in a more academic and historically correct interpretation of Italian architectural features. These tended to be monumental in scale, with correctly proportioned ornamentation of imported stone. Residential examples typically have a low-pitched roof concealed by a balustrade or cornice, liberal use of classical features, tall windows, ornate interior plasterwork, and heavy rustication. Italian Renaissance houses were more closely modeled on true Italian prototypes made possible with increased travel and Grand Tours, where clients could study the ancient classics and Renaissance architecture, and with an influx of Italian masons and craftsmen into the United States.

Charleston's best examples are found in late Victorian residential areas near Colonial Lake, along South Battery, and on Murray Boulevard. The Giovanni Sottile House (discussed below) is one of the finest in the city. The other prime example, the Villa Margherita built in

1895 at 4 South Battery, actually served as a model for Sottile's updates to his house on Rutledge Avenue.

The Villa Margherita at 4 South Battery on a 1921 postcard.

Antebellum Grand Tours

Elite South Carolinians interested in making a Grand Tour as a mark of their cultural refinement capitalized on the new ease of travel in the mid nineteenth century brought about by steam ships and rail within Europe. Maurie D. McInnis notes, "the enthusiasm for European works was due largely to the fact that in artistic taste, as in so many other matters, nineteenth century Charlestonians followed the lead of their British counterparts . . . when Charles Izard Manigault visited the palazzo of an unnamed prince in Rome in 1830, he commented that 'this modern prince would be glad to sell his paintings and statuary.'" Robert A. Leath explains in *Pursuit of Refinement* that, "many Charlestonians purchased souvenir works of art in Rome . . . and sought those Grand Tour experiences that would make them men and women "of great taste." Italy was the most obvious and important destination for Charlestonians who wished to hone their connoisseurship skills. Perhaps most suggestive of the emotive power of studying works of art in person is Charles Izard Manigault's assessment of the Neapolitan sculpture collection: "It is while viewing such specimens of the arts as these that we are gradually led on to admire what at first to us appears a cold and inanimate art and end in coinciding in the conviction that marble can be made almost 'to speak'."

Naples and Pompei became very popular with tourists by the nineteenth century, and both Alicia Middleton and Charles Manigault visited. Charles ultimately made five trips to Italy between the 1830s and the 1850s and brought home several pieces, including *Madonna of the Apple*, purchased from the collection of Carlo Cignani (a leading 17th century artist in Parma). He visited the Naples region on his first trip and brought home a series of gouaches of the region, one featuring Mount Vesuvius. Elite Charlestonians also flocked to Florence and Rome on their Grand Tours to visit the collections of the Old Masters at the Vatican and Musei Capitolini and the Tribuna in Florence (where the *Venus de Medici* was a favorite.) Charlestonian Francis Kinloch was living in Florence at the time to study sculpture, and "often acted as a guide and companion to visiting friends from Charleston."

William and Harriet Aiken amassed an impressive collection during their Grand Tour to Europe in 1857-1858, including a bandit scene purchased from Prince Torlonio's gallery in Rome, *Flight Into Egypt* by Carlo Marratti, a copy of *Proserpine* by Hiram Powers, and a reduced scale copy of Canova's *Venus italica*. Of the Venus, Maurie McInnis notes, "the original sculpture was completed in 1802, and it was immensely popular with those on the Grand Tour. No fewer than six full size copies were commissioned from Canova during his lifetime. After his death, other sculptors in Florence continued to produce copies." William Aiken purchased a new commission by a Florentian sculptor called *The First Grief*, in addition to the master copies, showing a broad interest in Italian art. Mrs. Aiken purchased books on the tour to further educate herself on the masters, such as *Sacred and Legendary Art and Biographical Catalogue of the Principal Italian Painters*. Several of Aikens' pieces are on display in the restored 1850s art gallery of the Aiken Rhett House, operated by the Historic Charleston Foundation.

Maurie McInnis notes that, "Charleston had several antebellum exhibitions to display copies of the masters, such as *Madonna della Seggiola*, copied after Raphael, which was brought from Italy. There were several copies of this painting in Charleston; most of the city's collectors owned one. As Charles Izard Manigault commented when visiting the Pitti Palace in Florence where the original was displayed, "I was most delighted that the Madonna painted by Rafael which we often see in the United States where we called it the 'Madonna' as if there was but one Madonna as a painting known . . . Uncle Smith had this copied when in Italy 25 years ago and it is a most charming copy of this enchanting picture." More than ten percent of the Carolina Art Association's exhibition pieces in Charleston between 1858 and 1861 were Italian baroque area masterpieces.

CHAPTER 4:

INCREASED ITALIAN IMMIGRATION IN POSTBELLUM CHARLESTON

Immigration from Italy increased in the years after the Civil War, as people sought to escape rural poverty, political unrest, and the aftermath of several serious earthquakes that wracked mainland Italy and Sicily. Father Richard C. Madden, historian of the Catholic Church in the state, noted, "the immigration of Italians to the state becomes noticeable in the early 1870s. By 1871 there were enough in Charleston to form an Italian society. There is no indication, however, that [Italian Jesuit Father Aloysius Louis] Folchi was active in the group. The society seems to have centered itself around St. Joseph's parish and the society which was formed in 1871 took the name St. Joseph's Latin Society. The patron's feast day, St. Joseph's Day, in 1876, fell on a Sunday. The *News and Courier* for March 20th reported in full on the parade that marched from Hibernian Hall to Broad Street to East Bay on to Market to Meeting, continued onto Wentworth-then to Anson Street to St. Joseph's where the "sons of sunny Italy" were addressed by the pastor, Charles Croghan, on "aspects of Italian history."

St. Joseph's Catholic Church (now St. Johns Reformed Methodist Episcopal) on Anson Street.

Following the American Civil War, Charleston's black majority included freed people moving to the city looking for work as they fled the plantations. David Gleeson notes, "these racial demographics scared many South Carolina leaders. The post–Civil War period saw an increase in official interest in immigration. Not since colonial times had South Carolina had such a major government effort to attract foreign immigrants. The impetus for these efforts was the desire to replace black labor." In 1881, the General Assembly established a Bureau of Immigration, which advertised in New York City for immigrants to come to South Carolina, and even organized cheap transportation to bring them to the state. It is important to remember, however, that the state actively recruited northern Europeans, who were preferred over those from the south. Governor Ben Tillman, a known and vehement racist, was one of the loudest spokesmen against recruiting Italian immigrants to settle in South Carolina, and "openly condemned attempts to recruit southern European, especially Italian, immigrants." Nonetheless, hundreds did arrive in South Carolina and many found their way to the Lowcountry.

As more immigrants settled in Charleston, the diversity of the Catholic Church expanded, and several new congregations formed. St. Peter's, founded at 34 Wentworth Street in a former Jewish synagogue by Bishop Patrick Lynch, is an example. It was primarily founded to serve the African American community, and Father Folchi was the first pastor. He founded St. Peter's School in the adjacent building. He left St. Peter's to serve as priest in the upstate, where he was a missionary to the Catawba tribe, before leaving for California to settle in a new Jesuit mission in 1877.

With the increasing Italian population, the position of Italian consul, whose charge is to protect, assist, and to advocate for the citizens of one's country in another nation, became ever more important. Italian consuls carried out fundraising to aid Italians in Charleston as well as in the mother country, encouraged business connections, and acted as spokesmen for the culture and character of their people. For example, Antonio Castellano, who served in the 1880s, asked "Italians residing in Charleston and the citizens of this city for assistance for the sufferers by the recent earthquake in Italy. The press has given such full details of the loss of life and property that I do not think it necessary to go into this, but earnestly ask for help on behalf of my unfortunate countrymen. Contributions will be received at my office, 9 Atlantic Wharf" in 1887.

34 Wentworth Street, formerly St. Peter's Catholic church and school.

Commercial merchants' buildings along Atlantic wharf.

Although the grocery industry in Charleston was dominated by Germans and native-born Charlestonians, many Italians entered the field as well, possibly using their connections to the Old World to import goods. Operating a small shop or grocery cart took a limited investment, which might be why this type of business was so common with newly arrived immigrants, who could later work towards a larger storefront as they profited. The 1910 *City Directory* listed both Vincent Chicco and N. Garbini with large grocery establishments in the Market. Mr. Pietro Vignolo operated a restaurant at 44 North Market Street at that time as well. Vignolo was a much-loved resident, eulogized upon his death in August 1910:

> "Well known Italian laid to rest- noted for kindness. The funeral service over the late Mr Pietro Vignolo [who] was one of many prominent Italians in Charleston, having conducted a restaurant at 44-46 Market Street for a number of years. He came to Charleston in his early youth and built up a solid business through his energy and enterprise. His kindness to the poor, especially to his own countrymen, is well known throughout the city and that state, hundred having been given a 'lift' in time of need through his liberality. He was a member of the Latin Society and is survived by a widow."

Vignolo's death certificate, on which Vincent Chicco was the witness, stated that he was born in 1862 in Italy. His wife Sophia was fourteen years his junior and was also Italian. A brief look at the Vignolo family in the 1900 census on Market Street shows that the area was a true ethnic enclave of Italians, Germans, and Portugese residents. Giaccomo Vignolo, a 42-year-old fruit dealer, lived one door down with his German wife Wilhelmina. Other neighbors on the block of Market between Church and East Bay Street included fruit dealer Charles Esponito and his wife Concetta; peddler Abhramio Joseffi and his wife Sophia; and peddler Joseph Soca, his wife Rosina, and several of their children.

The 1900 U.S. Census shows several Italian families in the Market.

Italian Farmers

Many Italians coming to Charleston, especially those from Sicily and the southern regions, had been farmers or farmhands in their home country, and sought similar work in the Lowcountry. They faced labor competition in South Carolina, where heavily exploited African Americans filled most tenant farming and sharecropping positions. Some agricultural societies in the South touted southern European laborers as a possible answer to labor shortages as black workers began to move to cities for other opportunities or sought to start their own small farms. Two articles in the *News and Courier*, "Italian Immigrants" and "Bring on the

Italians," in June 1904 illuminated local attitudes toward Italian farm workers: "We have always thought that the discrimination against Italians in the law establishing our state bureau of agriculture unjust and unwise, and as time goes on and the experience of the bureau increases, we are more and more confirmed in that view. We published yesterday a letter from Prof. Von Fingerlin, who brought a colony of Italians here in Reconstruction days. Most of the colonists got to work in Columbia, but the reign of the carpet bagger, scalawag, and negro was not favorable to white immigrants, and that experiment failed. All that is changed now, and Prof. Fingerlin agrees with us that the Italian agriculturalist is a good laborer, industrious, frugal, temperate, courteous, easily satisfied, and above all, adapted to the climate of the South." "Bring on the Italians" noted that an "influx of Italians" could fill local labor shortages and "in a few years the Italian immigrants would become the American citizen, and assimilated into our body politic, would be an active vital force in the large development of the industrial and commercial interests of this commonwealth."

In 1909, Alberto Pecorini wrote of Italian farm work in the south: "to sum up, the Italians as agricultural laborers have given remarkably good results in almost every locality, especially where the climate is mild and where they can soon become landowners. If it is asked why then the Italians have not become agricultural laborers in larger proportions, I answer that at the time of their coming agriculture is not so inviting a proposition as industrial work. They are practically penniless on landing and need to work not for the distant future but for the immediate present. Among those who already have their families here, who are relieved of the anxiety of the future, who have saved a little and have learned something of the laws and the spirit of the land there are undoubtedly many who would prefer the independent and healthy life of the country to the dependent and unhealthy life of the city. But in all cases the agricultural proposition must be laid before them fairly; they must not see exploitation where others speak of colonization, and in every way, they must have fair play."

Giovanni Sottile, in his quest to find gainful employment for his fellow immigrants, established a model farm in Ladson, South Carolina, managed through his Gangi Progressive Agricultural and Industrial Society, which employed Italians exclusively. By 1905, ten Italians were experimenting with mulberry trees for cultivating silk, and several other experimental crops. This, however, was one of few successful farm colony ventures in the Charleston area.

Italian Small Businesses: Fruit Merchants

While Italians were found in most facets of Charleston employment, they made up a notable portion of the city's fruit dealers and merchants. Beyond peddling with small carts, these men and women had businesses of their own that were listed in the *City Directories,* and some operated at one location for decades, demonstrating stability. Out of 81 such businesses in 1901, 13 were owned by Italian immigrants (one of whom was a widowed young woman.) There was also a notable amount of Greek fruiterers listed. The Italian business owners are listed below at their 1901 locations, with life spans and country of origin identified using South Carolina death certificate and census data where available. Notably, Marx "Michael" Elmero, born in Naples, operated a shop at 165 Calhoun Street at least from 1900, until his death in 1959. G. D. Guida is discussed in detail in a later chapter of the book.

- Gatano Cafiero, (1849-1913), Captain. Merchant. Born in Italy. 213 King
- GT DiPaola, Italy, 99 Nassau
- Joseph DiYorio (1868-1917), born in Italy. 320 Meeting
- Marx "Michael" Elmero. (1872-1959). Born in Naples. Grocery store, 165 Calhoun at time of death, and in 1901.
- Charles Esposito. (1867-1938), merchant and fruit dealer. Central Market/ 45 Market Street
- Gaetano Esposito. (1857-1922) 127 Meeting, later 133 Queen.
- Anna Fontana (1860-1905.) Italy. 37 State
- GD Guida
- Joseph Gaunglia, 391 King
- Charles Mauro, 403 King
- Tom Minrio, 253 Meeting
- Annie Mollo (widow John Mollo). Italian. 133 Queen
- Andrew Verde (1840-1914), Italy. 611 King

Anti-Italian Sentiment and Immigrant Quotas

Governor Tillman continued his campaign to recruit immigrants in the first decade of the twentieth century, but not Italians. Ongoing prejudice against Italians and other southern Europeans as "swarthy" and culturally inferior led the State of South Carolina to actively seek immigrants from western and northern Europe instead, and in 1908, the state closed its immigration department. The *Charleston Evening Post* reported, "state statutes prevent the state commissioner soliciting Italians but others are active - Consul [Giovanni] Sottile is likely to bring more to his farm in Ladson. . . under the laws of South Carolina, the immigration commissioner is not permitted to solicit the immigration of people from southern Europe, so the Italian movement is restrained as far as active efforts from the state are concerned." Federal laws in the 1920s establishing a quota system furthered restrained immigration, although most Italians were attracted to the northern states anyway, where cities offered larger ethnic enclaves and cultural continuity, and where there were more entry level industrial jobs available.

CHAPTER 5:

IMPORTANT ITALIAN FAMILIES AT THE TURN OF THE CENTURY

Several Italian immigrants who arrived in Charleston either directly or by way of New York in the late nineteenth and early twentieth century became well-known and wealthy citizens of their new city. They made their fortunes with creative business ventures, and several ascended into local politics as well.

The Cantini Family

Anania Cantini was born in Pisa, Italy in 1850 and arrived in the United States with his brother, Geromio in 1874. The two set up a successful grocery and olive oil, wine, and liquor importation business in Charleston by 1877.

A Cantini ad from October 1877.

In 1887, Anania was operating a small grocery shop on Council Street, which became the setting for a shooting and ensuing murder inquest when Cantini shot an African American man named Robert Anderson in the shop, later determined to be in self-defense, on Christmas Eve. The *News and Courier* reported, "Cantini is a well-known Italian, and Anderson is equally well known, a sea faring man. Anderson allegedly threatened to kill Cantini's brother Peter after a fight had occurred between Anderson and another black man called Bailey, whom Anderson was sure was still hiding in the store. Anderson left at the instruction of the police, but returned that evening with a knife, and Cantini drew his pistol and shot him before he could advance. Cantini was held at the police station before the coroner's inquest the next day. Witnesses described him as "a peaceful, law abiding citizen, and the general prevailing opinion seems to be that he acted strictly in self-defense."

The brothers operated G and A Cantini general store, grocery, and saloon at the west end of Tradd Street, number 169, in the 1890s. The shop was on a small area of made land near the Ashley River marshes (which at that time stemmed inland to the vicinity of Savage Street). There was a small wharf next door where nearly 50 small boats docked each day to unload crops from the farms and former plantations on the Ashley River, including okra, tomatoes, corn, and melons. Geromio lived above the store, while Anania and his Irish American wife Sarah Mackin and their children lived at 52 King Street.

52 King Street, the home of Anania Cantini.

Anania was best known for his fight against the state Dispensary Laws, which stipulated that spirituous liquors, wines, and beers could only be imported and sold by state approved franchises. It was effectively a statewide prohibition law enacted under Governor Pitchfork Ben Tillman in the 1890s and met with much resistance, especially in Charleston. Several bootleggers, "blind tiger" (illicit pub) operators (such as famous Vincent Chicco, who is discussed below), and importers and grocers like Cantini were involved in clandestine liquor sales and tavern operation as they worked to skirt the laws. The Cantini Brothers embarked on a years-long court battle against Governor Tillman and the dispensary laws in March of 1893. Their firm, G&A Cantini, had been "doing business as importers and vendors of spirituous, vinon, and malt liquors" for years prior to the dispensary laws passed in December 1892. Their lawyers argued that as subjects of the Kingdom of Italy, the brothers should be protected by treaty stipulations protected by the US Constitution and therefore should be exempt from the dispensary importation laws. After nearly four years, they lost the suit in July of 1897.

Anania was more successful with his second court case, in which he sued the state for damages from an illegal search of his home on King Street, where four constables confiscated hundreds of bottles of old and rare Italian wine that Cantini had imported for his own use. The paper reported that on 4 October 1893, "A novel feature of the day's work was the searching of the private residence of Cantini, in King Street. In this was found a cellar full of rare old Italian wines, the private property of Cantini, who has been importing wine for years, and does not sell it. There was at first a promise of resistance when the constables attempted to enter the house, but the owner finally permitted the search . . . The constables raided the house believing that it contained liquors belonging to Vincent Chicco". In each establishment they raided that day, "the doors were taken off their hinges, glasses, bottles, and bar room fixtures of every kind were confiscated, and of course, every kind of liquor was carried off to jail." Cantini had the four constables (Gaillard, Pepper,

IMPORTANT ITALIAN FAMILIES AT THE TURN OF THE CENTURY

Swan, and McDonald) charged with conspiracy and malicious trespass, and contended that he, his brother, and their families were assaulted and harassed during the search of 52 King (the private residence) and 169 Tradd Street. Judge Simonton had the four arrested with chance for bail, and the case made its way slowly through the system. In April 1895, a headline stated, "Cantini Wins!" The court found in his favor and the state awarded him $3000.00 in damages.

169 Tradd Street, the site of Cantini's stores.

The brothers continued operating their shop on Tradd Street after the legal battles. Geromio died in 1904 at age 60 at his brother's house on King Street, of chronic nephritis. Anania and Sarah moved to Sullivan's Island, where they opened a new grocery. Anania died in 1915 of heart failure and was interred at St. Lawrence Catholic Cemetery in Charleston. Sarah died in 1941 on Sullivan's Island and is presumably buried next to her husband, although only she has a headstone at St. Lawrence.

Vincent Chicco: Politician, Anti-Prohibitionist

Vincent Chicco was born in Italy in 1851. He left his native country as a young man to become a sailor, and upon docking in Charleston he decided to remain. Chicco became a citizen in 1874, worked as a grocer, and as was typical of the era, he also had a saloon in his shop. During state-wide prohibition, Chicco became a bootlegger of some notoriety and operated a "blind tiger." He was a good friend of Mayor John Grace, a workingman's politician who was pro-immigrant and anti-prohibition. Chicco served as a city councilman and was a strong supporter of Grace during both of his non-consecutive mayoral terms. Chicco's son, Vincent Jr., was also a successful real estate developer and entrepreneur in Charleston.

Vincent Chicco and his family in the 1900 census.

IMPORTANT ITALIAN FAMILIES AT THE TURN OF THE CENTURY

Chicco actively solicited to bring Italian immigrants into Charleston for work opportunities. For example, in 1904, 22 arrived in the city on a Clyde Line ship to take posts at the Charleston Navy Yard, which Chicco secured for them. The local paper noted, "Mr. Chicco took his fellow countrymen in his charge the moment they landed in South Carolina, introduced them to sunny Italy's Charleston colony and there was a happy reunion. Mr. Chicco is actively interested in bringing Italian immigrants to this state and expects next week to report the arrival of 175 more. There is one thing about South Carolina they don't like, and that is the wine. It is too strong and an Italian wine is to him what a cup of coffee or tea is to a South Carolinian. If my people could get the sort of wine they are accustomed to and get it without much trouble and expense, why, lots more of them would settle in this state and make good citizens."

Chicco operated a series of successful grocery and restaurant enterprises. His first establishment was located on North Market Street. By 1920, he had expanded with Chicco's Delicatessen (operated by the Cockino Brothers) at 209 King Street, which specialized in olive oil, olives, cheese, spaghetti, and Italian, Greek, French, and Spanish delicacies. He also owned 216 King Street, now called the McBride Chicco building. Historic Charleston Foundation notes, "Chicco apparently added the pressed-metal decoration to the building, including the semicircular window hoods and bracketed entablature and arched parapet."

Vincent Chicco and his saloon and grocery in Market Street, from a historic postcard.

A savvy businessman and investor, Chicco is probably best known for his role as a "blind tiger" operator. His notorious exploits are summarized in a biographical sketch provided by a namesake Italian restaurant, Vincent Chicco's, which today operates from a historic former warehouse building between Hutson and John Streets, next to the Hampton Inn that began as the Art Deco style Chicco Apartments, developed by Vincent Chicco Jr.:

> "During the prohibition era, Vincent Chicco became known as 'the king of blind tigers.' During this era, many Charlestonians considered themselves immune from the laws governing the rest of the state. Chicco ran a number of saloons in Charleston and led the fight locally against prohibition, where he was seen as a local hero. The secret behind the 'blind tigers' is one would pay to "see the blind tiger" (which of course didn't exist) and in exchange would receive a "free" drink. Vincent Chicco's illegal drinking establishments also caused him to become the first arrest after Governor Ben Tillmans's dispensary bill passed. Many Charlestonians opposed the state dispensary law, which encouraged Gov. Tillman to make Charleston "the driest place on earth". Vincent Chicco's arrest became infamous, and other barkeeps were reportedly jealous of his instant fame. Despite his brush with the law, he continued to sell alcohol to his customers and lead to at least three more arrests.

216 King Street, one of Vincent Chicco's buildings.

IMPORTANT ITALIAN FAMILIES AT THE TURN OF THE CENTURY

THE BRILLIANT SIGN CO.

COMMERCIAL WORK

OF ANY DESCRIPTION

"SIGNS THAT ARE FIT TO READ"

119 King Street

J. F. McLAUGHLIN

SANITARY PLUMBING AND HEATING

REPAIR WORK A SPECIALTY

ESTIMATES CHEERFULLY GIVEN

54 ANSON STREET   Phones 2439 and 2145-W

Phone 212   ESTABLISHED 1890   C. COCKINOS, Mgr.

THE CHICCO'S DELICATESSEN

COCKINOS BROS., Successors

PURE FOOD STORE

Oriental and Domestic Products

OUR SPECIALTIES—Pure Olive Oil, Olives, Cheese, Spaghetti
DELICACIES—Italian, Greek, French, Spanish

209 KING STREET   CHARLESTON, S. C.

EDWIN G. HARLESTON

Funeral Director

Phone 580-W

121 CALHOUN STREET   CHARLESTON, S. C.

CAFETERIA

TOBACCO, AND CIGARS, SODA WATER and CANDY

Quality and Premier Chocolates   Foss-Boston

Phone 3982

13 Broad Street   Charleston, S. C.

"GILT EDGE INVESTMENTS"

Every Policy issued by the State Life Insurance Company, of Indiana, is secured by a Deposit of the Full Legal Reserve with the Auditor of State. Twenty Million Dollars deposited with Auditor of State for the sole protection of Policyholders, giving you an investment and a protection that is absolutely secure. Your premiums will be paid during total disability by the Company, and in addition you will receive an income for life or until recovered, and in addition, the full amount of insurance will be paid to your beneficiary at your death, or to you at the maturity of your contract. INSURE TODAY.

THE STATE LIFE INSURANCE CO.

WM. C. SMITH, District Supervisor

240 Calhoun Street   Charleston, S. C.

Phone 144

EVERY MAN AND WOMAN IN CAROLINA SHOULD CARRY AN ENDOWMENT POLICY

ATTENTION! EVERYBODY!

List Your Properties FOR SALE or TO RENT With

CANNON & RODOLPH

Real Estate and Rentals—Loans Negotiated

Phone 3803   CALHOUN Cor. ST. PHILIP ST.

Chicco's Delicatessen advertised in the 1920 *Charleston City Directory*.

Chicco died in October 1928 and the *News and Courier* provided a short eulogy of his interesting and full life: "Chicco Funeral This Afternoon, Last Tributes to Be Paid City Alderman - Colorful Career Ended. The funeral of Vincent Chicco, alderman from ward 3, who died at his home 35 Hasell St. Wednesday afternoon will be conducted at St. Mary's Roman Catholic church at 3 o'clock this afternoon by the Rev. B. F. Fleming. Interment under the direction McAlister's will be at St. Lawrence cemetery. Alderman Chicco was serving his fifth term in city council as representative of ward 3. He had served under Mayor Grace during two terms, under Mayor Hyde, and under both terms of Mayor Stoney. There was almost never opposition against him at election time, and his many political and personal friends referred to him as the "mayor of ward 3." His life was one of adventure: Sailor, policeman, restaurant proprietor, and politician, he had seen much in his 78 years. Coming from Italy as a boy, he had been a resident of Charleston for sixty years. but he had tasted of life even before he came here. At 15, he shipped on an Italian brig. Yellow fever broke out, and all hands died save Mr. Chicco and the cook. This was a beginning of an adventurous career. In Charleston, he was at one time a railroad employee, again a member of the police force, and then for many years he operated a widely celebrated restaurant on Market Street. Possessed of a forceful personality and being a raconteur of ability, Mr. Chicco was one of the most colorful and best-known figures in Charleston up to the time of his death."

Vincent Chicco and his wife Mary Ann's headstone at St. Lawrence Cemetery

City Council remembered him kindly in a 1928 memorial honoring his service as alderman from 1911 until his death and noted that, "he evidenced an appreciation of the responsibilities and duties of the office by punctual and regular attendance and a careful and earnest consideration of public questions; not only in public life but in the commercial and civic activities of Charleston, Mr. Chicco rendered loyal service. The Council sincerely regrets that he is no longer to participate in the deliberations of this body." Vincent Chicco Jr. (1889-1957) carried on the family business and operated a wine and spirits wholesale distribution shop, specializing in imported goods. He and his wife Pearl Fincher resided in Mount Pleasant.

The Sottile Family

The Sottile family's experience after immigrating to Charleston is a true story of success. Salvatore Giovanni, a locksmith, ironworker, and Italian revolutionary, and his wife Rosina had several children, all born in Gangi, Sicily. All seven of their children: Giovanni, Nicholas, Santo, Albert, and James, followed later by Joseph and Marie, moved to Charleston. Rosina eventually came to Charleston as well and stayed for the remainder of her life in the city with her daughter Marie. Joseph returned to Sicily and James moved to Florida, but the other brothers remained in Charleston and became important politicians and business leaders.

IMPORTANT ITALIAN FAMILIES AT THE TURN OF THE CENTURY

The Sottile Brothers business circular. Courtesy of Sottile Family Reunion. Nick Sottile has added Nicholas Sottile into the circular (see top row, right side.)

Nicholas Sottile (1868-1928) arrived in New York in 1890 intending to head to South America. However, he received a message from his brother John in Charleston and instead came to South Carolina. He worked on a lighthouse tender and then briefly returned to Italy, where he married Maria Sottile. The couple returned to Charleston and Nicholas opened a restaurant called Washington Square Café, known for its European fare. When his wife passed away, he returned to Gangi, where he eventually remarried to Josephine Randazzo. They moved back to Charleston in 1906 and Nicholas founded a retail China and glassware emporium on King Street, while serving as a City Councilmen and investing in real estate, with great success. He had several children, Rosina, Luci, Mari, Nicholas, Frank, and Salvatore (by his first wife Mari, who died young, and his second wife, Josephine.)

Sottile served on the city's Ways and Means Committee, was chairman of the Committee on Education, and was a trustee of Charleston High School. He advocated for industrial education and championed vocational schools for Charleston. He founded the Italian Protective Society, which published articles that were sent to Italian papers during World War One to help offset the German, anti-American propaganda flooding into the country at that time. Mayor Grace said of Nicholas: "Mr. Sottile is a man of great worth. The Society is fortunate in having him as its head and Charleston is fortunate to have secured such a worthy citizen. He is a friend of the people of his land and has proven a friend to his adopted country and city." The City Council honored him upon his death in November of 1928 with a eulogy in the *City Yearbook,* which outlined his time as alderman for ward 4 from 1919 to 1923, "his useful and faithful public service to the City of Charleston", and his importance in the business community. In his passing, "the city has lost a valued citizen who served their interests in public and private life."

Charlotte Street, Nicholas Sottile's home.

Santo Sottile (1870-1931) arrived in 1894 after serving four years in the Italian army. He joined the Sottile Brothers firm in Charleston and worked in wholesale with his brother John after the partnership dissolved. He next opened his own Cadillac dealership, and had exclusive retail agency for the whole state, opening showrooms in Columbia and Greenville. Santo was also involved in several of his brothers' businesses. He retired from the Cadillac Co. in 1929 to take over management of the Charleston Hotel for his brother James, who had moved to Florida. Carmelina Sottile Thompson writes that, "Mr. Sottile was a keen businessman, plain and frank in his views, who could be counted upon to give sound advice when it was sought. His liberal disposition and congeniality made him a large circle of friends."

Santo Sottile in 1901 in his Charleston Exposition annual pass photograph. Charleston Archive, CCPL.

James Sottile (1887-1964) arrived in the United States in 1899 and became a naturalized citizen in 1913. James developed the Pastime Amusement Company before turning its management over to Albert Sottile. He then purchased the Charleston Hotel and was instrumental in developing the Isle of Palms. A shrewd real estate mogul, he was also involved in the development of Hampton Park Terrace and the neighborhoods near the Navy Yard in North Charleston. James married Louise Lillian, a South Carolinian of German descent, and worked as a broker and a public utility company manager before relocating to Florida. They had several children: Joseph, Albert J, Carolina, James, and Helen. In Florida, James purchased 20,000 acres of lowlands in 1924 about 30 miles from Miami and secured loans to drain the land and install streets to pave the way for development and agriculture. Sottile leased much of the land to northern farmers and grazed cattle. He became one of the most prominent cattle ranchers in Florida and had a citrus grove also. He founded the South Dade Farmers Bank, and donated lands to Dade County for a "migrant laborers camp" and for the creation of Biscayne Bay Park, which was dedicated to him in 1950.

Carmelina Thompson writes, "a man of progressive views, Mr. Sottile was always seeking new ways of improving his amazingly productive enterprise and the exceptional nature of his undertaking made it the subject of feature articles in Reader's Digest, Fortune Magazine, and other publications."

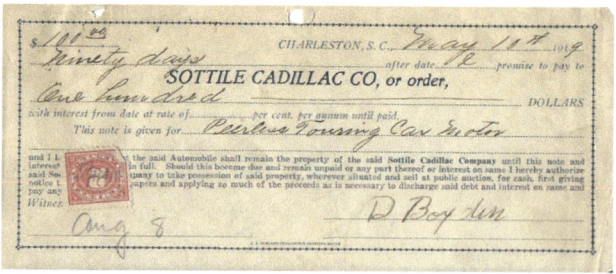

A receipt for a car from Sottile Cadillac. Courtesy of Sottile Family Reunion.

Albert Sottile (1878-1960) came to Charleston in 1891 at age 13. He was an office boy for the Commandant of the 6th District Lighthouse Department before joining the Pastime Amusement Company with his brother James. Albert became head of the company, which operated most of the theaters in the city. He helped develop Hampton Park Terrace, Wagener Terrace, Isle of Palms (even creating a company to run street cartrack to the island) and was the vice president of the lucrative Charleston Hotel Company. Albert's landmark Charleston theaters included the Gloria (later renamed the Sottile Theater on George Street), the Arcade, the American Theater on King Street, the Garden, the Avondale, and the fabulous Art Deco style Riviera Theater at King and Market Streets (all of which are extant and have been adaptively used as event spaces and commercial/retail spaces.) Albert also served on the Charleston Board of Development and the Port Utilities Commission.

The Gloria/Sottile Theater is now owned by College of Charleston, which lovingly restored it in 2019. A recent C of C article states that, "during intermission at the Gloria, when the 16-millimeter reels required changing, Mr. Sottile would entertain the crowds by singing Italian songs to them, all accompanied by a grand organ he had imported from Italy that was played by his secretary, Miss Dengate. The [painted wall] murals also paid tribute to Italy, through sweeping vistas of a Mediterranean seaside peopled with toga-draped muses of the arts. However, well before his granddaughters were old enough to attend the Gloria, the murals had been obscured by acoustic panels, which were eventually removed during a subsequent renovation."

The Gloria Theater in 1939 at the opening of "Gone with the Wind." College of Charleston Special Collections.

Albert and his wife Mary Ellen Hartnett (of Irish descent) had only one daughter, Alberta Sottile, who married J.C. Long, a noted South Carolina politician, successful developer, and founder of the Beach Company (which has since become one of the leading property development companies of the Southeast.) The couple had two daughters, Mary Ellen Long Way, and Joyce Carolyn Long Darby. In the late 1980s, the city converted a former Ashley River millpond into a recreational lake, which Mayor Riley named Alberta Sottile Long Lake. Mrs. Long was an avid gardener and benefactor of the City Parks Department and had been the driving force in convincing the City Council to turn the pond into a public amenity.

The Albert Sottile house, shortly after it was constructed for its first owner Samuel Wilson, in 1892. From A. Wittemann's *Charleston, SC. Illustrated.*

Marie Sottile and **Joseph Sottile** came to Charleston in 1901 with their mother Rosina following her husband Salvatore's death in 1895. Rosina married Professor Santo Restivo, the brother of Carmela Sottile (Giovanni's wife) in 1910 at 81 Rutledge Avenue. They traveled back and forth between Charleston and Italy before separating. Marie lived with her mother on Wentworth Street and Santo returned to Italy to become dean of a university in Gangi. Joseph left Charleston to study the priesthood at a seminary in Baltimore, Maryland but due to ill health, he ultimately returned to Italy, where he died young at a sanitorium in Palermo in 1917.

Consul and Model Sicilian: Giovanni Sottile

Perhaps the most successful of the brothers politically was Giovanni Sottile, who was born 1866 and studied mathematics in Palermo before moving to the United States in 1889. He and his wife, Carmela Restivo (whom he met in Italy) had four children, all born in Charleston: Salvatore, Rosina, Giovanni Jr., and Carmelina. Sottile was appointed Italian consul to Charleston in 1899 (his jurisdiction was eventually expanded to include all of North and South Carolina), and he was knighted with the title of chevalier by the King of Italy.

Giovanni Sottile with his knight's sword. Courtesy of Sottile Reunion.

Sottile became wealthy in real estate speculation and liquor importation, and he opened a bar and restaurant called the Jetty House on Sullivan's Island in 1895 with his brothers. He remodeled 81 Rutledge Avenue in the Italian Renaissance Revival style upon purchasing the house in 1905, adding his initials in an etched glass pane on the entry door and to the iron driveway fence. Sottile lived in the house and used it as the consulate until his death in 1913, and it is listed on the National Register of Historic Places. As the nomination notes, "Sottile was an advocate for the Italian community of North Carolina and South Carolina and successfully brought two peonage cases involving exploitation of Italian immigrants to court, and he was instrumental in promoting Italian culture and heritage in Charleston. Sottile was an active statesman and used the Sottile House to entertain Italian dignitaries and local politicians. Sottile was knighted by the Kingdom of Italy for his diplomatic service to the country in 1909." That year, he held a glamorous event at the house for the crew of the Italian ship *Etruria*, which had called to Charleston: "In July of 1909, the Italian ship *Etruria* was in Charleston and Sottile again hosted diplomatic events at his house. Sottile's daughter Carmelina remembered that while the *Etruria* was in port, "there were parties [at the house] all week." The newspaper reported that after a carriage ride to

IMPORTANT ITALIAN FAMILIES AT THE TURN OF THE CENTURY

the Country Club, "Consul Sottile will entertain the officers [of the *Etruria*], the officers of the Navy Yard, the officers at Fort Moultrie, the city authorities, and especially invited guests. The following invitations have been issued: Cavaliere Giovanni Sottile, Royal Consulate Agent of Italy, requests the honor of your presence at a Smoker [men's only evening party with drinks and cigar smoking] to be tendered to Captain Count Leonardi Di Casalino and officers of His Majesty's Ship the *Etruria*." The *Evening Post* offered more details: "the concluding function of the stay will take place tonight in the form of a smoker at the elegant mansion of Consul Sottile on Rutledge Avenue. The lower piazza of the residence, and the garden and lawn, has been especially wired for the occasion and with the decorations which have been provided, a fitting setting has been arranged for the occasion."

The Consulate, 81 Rutledge Avenue, home of Giovanni Sottile, who renovated the house in the Italian Renaissance Revival style in 1905.

The Italian Laborer's Experience in late nineteenth century Charleston

The Sottile family's story of success was not typical of the Italian immigrant experience in Charleston, or in most American cities. The majority who arrived were unable to speak English, were Catholic (making them a target of suspicion in the majority-Protestant South), were economically disadvantaged on arrival, and were often viewed as a non-white race. Many experienced prejudice in their first decades in the United States, and they were often forced to take low paying labor jobs until they assimilated. Agents recruiting labor for industrial companies and large farms preyed upon Italian, Jewish, Irish, and Greek immigrants coming into New York, enticing them to the South on the promise of work and temperate climates. The National Register for the Sottile house notes, "In the early 1880s, Charleston Mining and Manufacturing Company (and its northern financiers) led an effort to import Italian workers from New York as replacements for local black laborers. In 1884, for example, a N. Gabrini of 26 Market Street advertised in the Charleston newspapers for "one thousand Italians wanted for employment on phosphate lands," producing fertilizer from the naturally occurring phosphate mined in the area. Though the phosphate labor force remained predominantly black, an Edisto Islander of the postbellum era remembered "a rough crowd of Irish, Italians, and Colored" mining workers."

ITALIANS IN THE LOWCOUNTRY

An 1884 advertisement placed by Gabrini soliciting Italian laborers to work in phosphates.

In the 1880s, phosphate companies experimented with Italian labor to potentially replace the black labor force, and some companies actively worked to import Italians coming into New York for their industry, while others preferred local African American labor. A March 1884 *News and Courier* article entitled, "There's Millions in it - the phosphate mines of South Carolina," enumerated the size and scope of the immigrant labor force at several local companies. Klett's Mill employed 240 miners, 180 of whom were Italian. At the Lambs mine, "300 [workers] are Italians and the rest are negroes. This is the third winter the Italians have been tried and they have given satisfaction. They are worked in separate fields from the negroes. They are worked by Italian contractors, who are paid so much a ton by the company for mining and who in turn pay the laborers supplied by them. The laborers make about a dollar a day. They are steady workers and their diligence has a wholesome effect on the negroes." Magnolia Mine employed only African Americans; "Italian laborers were tried here last year and gave perfect satisfaction. They were paid last year $1.25 a day. A gang of 50 were brought from New York this year, an offer was made to pay them by the pit and not by the day, as last year, and they refused to work on these terms and left." Bulow and Rose mines each employed 60 Italian workers, and at Bolton, 25 Italians "drifted down to the mines from Charleston" and worked loading cars and rolling rock, but did not dig in the pits, as "last year 60 Italians were brought out from New York by this company, and paid $1.10 a day, but the digging was too deep in the ground and too wet for them. In other kinds of work they did and still do good and efficient work. The Italians and other laborers are furnished with houses by the company, but find their own furniture and rations." In total, 605 Italians were employed locally in the phosphate industry in 1884. Four years later, an Italian named John Tarquinia (who appears in no other local records) was arrested and found guilty of selling "liquor without a license to the Italians at the Charleston Mining Company."

1884 phosphate labor and profit report, "Negro, Italian, and Convict Laborers."

IMPORTANT ITALIAN FAMILIES AT THE TURN OF THE CENTURY

Phosphate mining activities near Charleston, in *Frank Leslie's Illustrated*, 1880.

The Italian experience in the phosphate industry surrounding Charleston is one of the most striking examples of immigrant hardship, brought to light by Giovanni Sottile in the early twentieth century. Sottile worked briefly as an accountant in the phosphate industry in South Carolina and witnessed the exploitation of Italian laborers, which left a great impression on him. While consul, he used his political power as consul to bring public attention to the exploitation, and he was directly involved in bringing several peonage cases to trial. In one such case in 1900 involving the Pon Pon Phosphate Mine on Edisto River, the Charleston papers reported, "according to the unfortunate Italians, who are lured to this city to the mines on the promise of good pay, they are restrained there by armed guards and compelled to work well or sick, under pain of beating or even death, if they refuse, and by an ingenious system they are kept always in the debt of the padrone." Padrone, which means boss or manager in Italian, was the term applied to unscrupulous labor brokers who sold immigrants into unfair labor contracts or peonage. One sick worker who could not return to work was shot dead for disobeying a work order. Sottile also brought evidence in a case against Bulow Phosphate Company in 1905 for peonage (a system of forced labor, where a worker is often kept in perpetual debt and not allowed to leave the plantation or facility.) The "bosses" who had kept several Italians in "virtual slavery" at starvation wages were ultimately convicted. Sottile also helped bring the South and Western Railway Company of North Carolina to court for its ill treatment of its Italian workers, one of whom was shot to death for attempting to ask for payment.

Giovanni Baptista Sanguinetti (aka John Sanguinett)

Giovanni Sanguinetti's (1851-1905) experience as a working-class laborer was typical for the Italian immigrant living in the city. Like many Italians who settled in Charleston, Giovanni arrived in New York first, in 1879. Reflecting the discrimination Italians faced as new immigrants, the 25-year-old Americanized his name to John Sanguinett. He worked as a longshoreman for the Clyde Steamship line, a popular job for Italian immigrants but not without its challenges. An International Longshoremen's Association history booklet notes that, "Italian immigrants were very commonly employed as longshoremen because they were willing to work for lower wages. This created a great conflict with the Irish, as they had a firm hold on the dock jobs. Many employers exploited this conflict so that they could take advantage of the Italians' working for a lower wage." Giovanni worked on the wharves unloading and loading cargo into ships, in an era where much of the work was still done by hand and with limited technology rather than cranes.

Many of the Italians who had been coerced to move to South Carolina by padrones to work as phosphate or farm laborers eventually moved to the City of Charleston from the countryside in search of better work and more autonomy. Most lived in a few block radius of the Market area, in short distance to dock work and other industrial activities. As in the antebellum era, there was a high concentration of Italians in Ansonborough (ward 3), and to the south of the market along Queen and Cumberland Streets, in what is now part of the French Quarter. The Bertocci, Ferillo, and Pierano families lived on Cumberland Street. Historian W. Scott Poole notes that the high number of immigrants in Charleston compared to other parts of the state led to political similarities with northern cities; "concentrations of Irish Catholics, Jews, Italians, and German Lutherans lived in wards 3, 5, 7, and 9, the Charleston neighborhoods north of Broad Street and east of King. They shared a lack of affection for the "South of Broad" elites who set the tone for Charleston society and dominated its municipal elections. These outsiders found their champion in John P. Grace, Charleston's first Catholic mayor."

CHAPTER 6:

ITALIANS IN THE CITY OF CHARLESTON IN THE EARLY TWENTIETH CENTURY

By the 1910s and 1920s, Charleston had several second-generation Italian Americans who operated successful local businesses, and more first-generation Italians continued to arrive in the city on the recommendations of relatives who had previously arrived or were attracted by the coastal location. The "Charleston Renaissance", a period of artistic, musical, preservation/architectural, and literary rebirth in the city in the inter-war period, attracted wealthy new residents with Italian spouses who purchased notable historic buildings in the city and plantations in the country to restore them as winter homes.

Princess Pignatelli and the Preservation Movement

Henrietta Guerard Pollitzer Hartford (later Pignatelli) was born in Charleston. She descended from an interesting lineage; her mother's side, the Guerards, were of an elite colonial family, while her father was an Austrian Jew who emigrated in the 1860s. Henrietta married millionaire Edward Hartford after meeting him on a ship from Palm Beach to New York, and the couple had two children before his untimely death in 1922. She later met and married Prince Guido Pignatelli (nineteen years her junior and newly divorced, a double scandal for the era). Pignatelli was the son of General Pompeo dei Duchi di Montecalvo and Princess Helene Pignatelli, and eventually he became the Duke of Montecalvo, Marquess of Paglieta, Marquess of San Marco Locatola.

"Princess Pignatelli", whose friends simply knew her as Henrietta, spent much of her later life in the Charleston area, and she and Prince Guido lived at Wando Plantation in the 1940s, where they built an elaborate 32-room mansion replete with a nine-hole golf course. A true Lowcountry denizen, she was always interested in historic preservation. In 1933, she donated funds to the Charleston Museum that allowed them to purchase the Joseph Manigault house, saving it from demolition. Jonathan Poston explained, "by 1922 the financially distressed Preservation Society sold the property to Mrs. Ernest Pringle, who attempted valiantly to secure its future, reluctantly selling the garden to Standard Oil for a filling station. The gatehouse became a comfort station, and purchasers of full tanks of gas could receive free tours of the house. When the property was auctioned for default of a mortgage, the Museum purchased it with funds from Henrietta Pollitzer, Princess Pignatelli." 350 Meeting Street is still a house museum today and has been fully restored.

Henrietta died in 1948 and left the prince little inheritance while favoring her children. The prince left the Lowcountry shortly after her death and remarried. Princess Pignatelli, a Charlestonian with a noble Italian title, remains an important figure in early preservation initiatives in the city. She is buried at Magnolia Cemetery on the Cooper River marshes.

The Joseph Manigault house in the late 1970s, after the gas station had been removed. Historic American Buildings Survey, Library of Congress.

Italian restaurants and 20th Century businesses

Several first and second-generation Italians in the city followed the success of Chicco and Sottile and established their own restaurants, sometimes featuring Italian cuisine exclusively, while others offered a more eclectic fare. In 1930, two such Italian owned restaurants were Joseph Le Torre's short-lived establishment at 24 Inspection Street (he was listed as a welder and boiler maker in the 1920 census and was a second-generation Italian) and John Onorato's restaurant "opposite the Gulf Refining Company, on Cooper River." Onorato was born in Italy and married South Carolina-born Lula Lancaster. The restaurateur and his family lived on Chicora Place at the Navy Yard on the Charleston Neck with their children, J. Frank, Rose, Leona, Angelina, and Jenny. John's death certificate in July 1943 indicated that he was naturalized, but was born in Pollina, Italy in 1883. At the time of his death by heart failure, the former restaurant man was employed as a bandmaster with the US Navy, and as a county policeman.

ITALIANS IN THE CITY OF CHARLESTON IN THE EARLY TWENTIETH CENTURY

Little Italy restaurant at Cumberland and State Street.
Courtesy of Historic Charleston Foundation Archives.

Reflections from Giosue Guida, 1956, on early twentieth century Charleston

Naples native Giosue Guida (1880-1967) came to Charleston with his family as a young boy. In 1890, he purchased the 1780s house at 105 East Bay Street, and operated the Guida family grocery store in the building until the 1960s, while living above the shop. He added a pressed metal storefront and window cornices, and the entablature still bears the name "Guida," reminding passerby of the building's historic owner. In the fall of 1956, an Italian journalist Luigi Giarusso was in Charleston briefly working for the *News and Courier* while on an assignment with the United States Information Agency. He had a chance encounter with Guida, and decided to write a story of their discussion in a column for the paper. It is a rare glimpse into the experiences of an Italian immigrant who had spent most of his life in Charleston, and is filled with descriptions of the city in the past (taken from the *Courier,* 16 November 1956):

"Charleston," [Guida] said with unexpected vivacity, "was one of the most important ports in America, when the Indians were still in possession of Manhattan Island and New York was not yet a city. My father landed here with his ship in 1885 in order to load cotton and resin. He instantly fell in love with this city . . . Naturally, I also was born in Italy. We have not yet introduced ourselves: My name is Giosué Guida: one of the few Italians of the first generation here in Charleston… I was born near Naples, in Serano, on the peninsula of Sorrento. I arrived here as a child and during this time ships were entering this harbour by the hundreds from all countries of the world. Do you see this street so elegant? Half a century ago it was covered with cotton. We were walking as on carpet. Many ships had to lie at anchor for 2 weeks or more to dock. The loading was very slow at that time and was effected by mule power… My father immediately fell in love with this city, and here opened a mercantile store specializing in ship supplies."

I asked him admiringly where he learned the Italian language so perfectly. "I started school in Italy, for a year or two. A month after my arrival in Charleston I was already speaking English enough to permit me to play with my companions, but in my family we spoke often in Italian. Here at school I had to work very hard in the beginning in order to keep up with my colleagues. Later it was rather easy for me at high school, where I received my diploma."

In conversation we arrived at his home at 105 East Bay Street. It gave me the impression of entering in a museum of precious memories: photographs, paintings, carpets, furniture, cut glasses, china spoke of the splendid adventure of Captain Giovani Domenico Guida and his son Giosué, who left the enchanting coast of Sorrento to conquer a new world full of promises. Unconsciously I lowered my voice, when I was making my inquiries, as if I feared to profane the sublime silence of that home.

"Everything is as it was," Mr. Guida said, looking up for some old photographs mellowed by age, in an album covered with precious blue velvet. "This is Captain Cafiero, from Sorrento, this is Captain X, this is Captain Z, this is Captain Carlo Mauro. The latter is still one of the most popular exponents of our small Italian colony in Charleston, including Mr. Alberto Sottile and a few others. We were all members of the famous Society "Sons of Italy in America," which succeeded the "Latin Society of Union and Protection." I was president of this Society known as venerable."

In an old photograph still quite clear a young man dark haired and determined but serious and composed attracted my attention. I asked who this person was and he said, "That is me at the time that I received my diploma" [from Charleston High School]. I asked him what was the medal on his breast. For the first time Mr. Guida appeared to hesitate. "It is the Colcock Medal," he said, and I had to insist to get some details. I gathered in this way that this represents one of the most coveted awards for the students of Charleston. In fact this medal is obtained not only by the merit of the student but also by the vote of the faculty and graduation class.

I then understood what this medal means to Giosué Guida, a foreign student in Charleston, selected from hundreds of companions. He hid his emotion opening the album of his memories: "In this room," he said, "have passed the most distinguished peoples of the Old Charleston. Mr. Carlo Mauro met his wife, Rosina Verdi, in this very room. His son, Captain Charles Mauro, is at present in charge of the second missile-carrier "Canberra." Mr. Giovanni Sottile aso passed through this room. He was on his way to Jacksonville. My father helped him to find employment in Charleston. At present the Sottile family is one of the most distinguished in the South."

"On this street," he added, showing me East Bay Street, from the window of his home, "has transpired a large part of the history of Charleston. Half a century ago we needed 3 policemen in two blocks, just to maintain order amongst the hundreds of sailors from all nations who were unloading here. Now one-half policeman would be enough. But probably it was more beautiful then: laughing, shouting, happy voices filled East Bay Street; at dawn the mariners would return to the ships tired, happy, and naturally a little gay. They would often lose, on this sort of cotton carpet, their coins (result of the beer). Some persons had a good time here searching for money in the cotton on the street. Maybe," Mr Guida said smilingly, "here was born the saying that in America everyone can find money on the streets. Evidently some foreign sailors had observed people searching amongst the cotton."

"In some of these houses which are now owned by aristocratic families of Charleston (and which at present are main attractions for the tourists) were located about a dozen taverns. They were not enough for the sailors who came ashore. I am writing a book on East Bay Street. A book of memories: the story of this street and each of these houses."

Mr. Guida hesitated for a moment and added, "I do not know whether it is opportune to publish this book. Perhaps it would not be in good taste to divulge that in the house X which is now occupied by a distinguished family of Charleston, half century ago French, Italian, English sailors would get drunk."

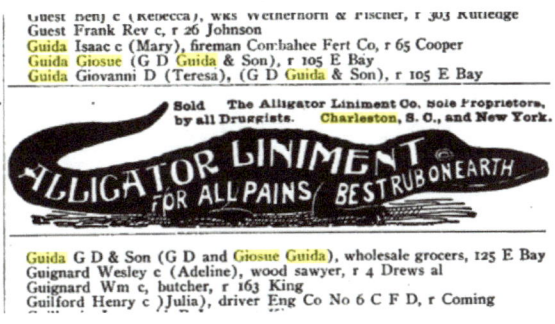

The Guida family in the *City Directory*.

It was very difficult for me to leave Mr. Guida, but evidently he needed to rest and also to rehearse the Verdi's Mass, which he was to sing in the morning. In fact Mr. Guida sings as basso, a privilege and hobby which no one would deny to an Italian. During the day he sells groceries; time past he supplied ships. At nights he shuts himself alone with his memories in the large home of his father Captain Giovan Domenico Guida, where everything recounts the story of courage of those who left their native land to bring to foreign shores the effort of their enthusiasm, their honest labor and (why not?) their passion for music, for singing and all that is beautiful."

Guida died in Charleston of heart failure in December 1967, at the age of 87, still residing at 105 East Bay Street. He was interred at St. Lawrence Catholic Cemetery.

Guida's Death Certificate.

CHAPTER 7:
WORLD WAR II TO THE LATE TWENTIETH CENTURY

As Europe descended into World War Two, Charleston's Italians reacted with dismay when Italy entered the war against the Allied powers on the side of Germany. Former Italian consul Carlos Mauro was interviewed about his thoughts on the war. Mauro was from Naples and like many local Italians, arrived in Charleston by way of New York City. He and his wife Rosa (also born in Italy) lived on Calhoun Street. He operated a barber supply business in which several of his children were employed. He had given up his position in 1927 when Mussolini ruled that only Italian citizens could serve as consul (Mauro had naturalized as a US citizen). He stated, "I have always been against war. My wish and prayer always has been for Mussolini to keep out of the war. I have no connection with the Italian government and am an American. If America goes to war with Italy, I myself and my son will go against the country of my birth. I love the country of my birth but in this case I have nothing to do with her; I am an American, and that is the expression of every Italian here."

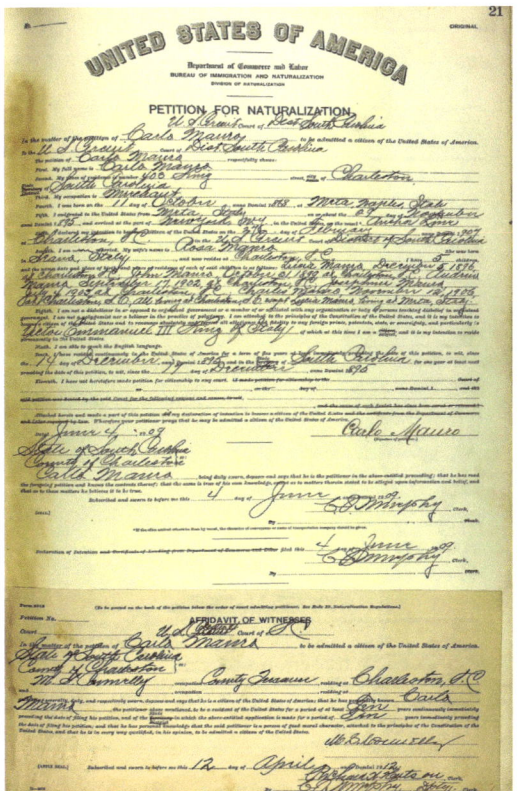

Mauro's application for U.S. citizenship, February 1907.

Similarly, Sam Convertino, president of the Christopher Columbus Lodge Sons of Italy chapter and owner of Convertino Shoe Factory told the *News and Courier* that, "I am against this war. If the dictators want to fight let them put all the higher ups in the field and let them shoot each other. I am a working man and most of the Italians are working men and we pay for the wars, not the higher ups." Sam was born in Bari, Italy in 1896, but he died young of heart failure in 1951. His sons John and Thomas also worked at the shoe repair factory and continued to operate it.

The State of South Carolina required aliens and foreign-born residents of the state to register, but there were no internment protocols or legal restrictions enacted against South Carolina's Italians.

During the war, approximately 115,000 German and Italian POWs were sent to the United States. South Carolina had twenty Prisoner of War camps in seventeen counties for Axis prisoners, including a small facility in West Ashley that began as an Italian encampment and later became a German internment facility. Historian John H. Moore noted that, "the story of Italian POWs [in America] is especially complex since Italy officially changed sides in 1943 and became an ally of the United States. How to treat ex-soldiers of an ex-enemy turned friend was a baffling question indeed." Nearby residents were at first apprehensive about the camps, where prisoners were put to work harvesting crops or cutting pulpwood, but Fritz Hamer notes, "it became clear that the vast majority of these prisoners were glad to be out of the war. They were getting three meals a day, and many liked having a different routine [working] out of the camps." Quarters were rudimentary and many prisoners lived in tents.

Many of the Italians arriving in Charleston were part of a service unit program designed to allow Prisoners of War who wished to defect from the Nazi cause to work in the military service sector on behalf of the allied forces. General James T. Duke, commander of the Charleston Port of Embarkation, was in charge of the local units and stated that the Italians were "saving thousands of dollars and performing work for which it was impossible to get civilian labor . . . it was found that many of the Italian POWs did not approve of the cause they had been fighting for and really wanted to participate actively against those that had forced the war upon them. These men were given an opportunity to volunteer for a service unit in which they agreed to work on behalf of the United States on any task except in actual combat." The port units consisted of one supervising American officer, four Italian officers, four American enlisted men, and 22 Italian enlisted men each. In the summer of 1944, they salvaged 1,500,000 board feet of lumber for the war effort. Duke explained to the local paper that, "[the Italians] are in a strange land and must be taught the customs and language. At the same time, the people in the community must be helped to understand the position of these soldiers. In the minds of many, they are still prisoners of war, but actually they are working for victory with us. Two special difficulties have arisen in respect to civilian communities in which these units have been placed. The attitude of over sympathy and its opposite, extreme hatred, antagonism, and insult. A special system has been evolved to permit the Italians to visit a community to practice Italian and English."

William Plyer wrote a brief story for the popular page, "Charleston History Before 1945", relayed to him by a Coast Guard seaman named Tony Agresta about his wartime experience at the Charleston guard station, who spoke fondly of the Italian POWs he met: "One morning Tony heard servicemen who could speak Italian were being solicited for escorting prisoners at the West Ashley POW camp. Tony had learned some Italian from his father as a kid so he volunteered. He drew a pistol from the armory, a big, heavy .45 caliber M1911A1. Agresta said he really hoped he wouldn't have to use it. Agresta drove a jeep up to the gate of the prison camp and met the group of prisoners he was to escort. To his surprise, the Italian prisoner who spoke the most English enthusiastically grinned and demanded, "We want to see Betty Gable," referring to the iconic 40's actress whose famous pin-up poster had been taken around the world by American servicemen. Agresta was a bit taken aback but he shrugged and gestured at his jeep saying, "Get in."

The Italians piled into Agresta's Jeep and he drove back toward downtown Charleston across the route 17 bridge over the Ashley River. The Coast Guardsman chatted with them and they quickly relaxed. His "prisoners" were clearly delighted to be out of the camp and just as clearly had no desire whatsoever to escape. Like many of their countrymen and even some Germans, they preferred an easy imprisonment in America to fighting what was becoming more and more evident a losing war. Agresta and his charges made quite an impression in downtown Charleston, drawing odd looks from other servicemen and girls promenading in sundresses. As per their request, he took them to a Betty Gable movie at one of the theaters on King Street. Feeling exuberant afterwards, he took them to one of his favorite restaurants and bought them dinner. When they finally got back to the base, he shook their hands and wished them well."

Early Interest in Italian Cuisine

La Brasca's Italian restaurant and pizzeria, operating at the corner of King and Cleveland Streets, served the northern neighborhoods of Charleston. Interestingly, they also served Chinese food, but were best known for their authentic red sauce. The building is no longer extant, and a parking lot is in its place today.

A postcard image of now-lost La Brasca's Italian Restaurant building, corner of Cleveland and King Streets.

In 1979, Charleston's Italians held a Columbus Day festival, which seems to have been a short-lived cultural event, but one that sought to bring Italian culture and fare to the city's residents, nonetheless. The *News and Courier* reported in October: "Italians in Charleston are paying homage in a big way to their forbear, Christopher Columbus. To honor his memory, Sunday's festival will feature exotic Italian foods, tarantella dancing and authentic Italian music. Throughout the day, Italian American club members will be busy cooking and selling such tempting treats as Italian sausage, meatballs and fried peppers, accompanied by pastries, confections, and espresso. Tickets may be purchased in advance at Dino's downtown and Tom Portaro's on Rivers Avenue."

Italian Owned Restaurants

In the last 40 years Downtown Charleston has counted three restaurants opened by proprietors born in Italy, as well as a gelato shop, all of which specialized in bringing authentic Italian cuisine to the Lowcountry.

La Pasta (1980-1994)

The restaurant La Pasta was opened in 1980 by a couple who moved directly from Italy to start a new chapter of their life. Lucia Pecetti and her husband Nik Zuccalà, left Milano for America, looking for a small town close to the sea. They ended up in Charleston and found the city the perfect locale for their plan to open a small romantic restaurant. They named it La Pasta, transforming an old sandwich place on Ashley Avenue, across from MUSC. La Pasta became a true Italian restaurant, open just for dinner, with white tablecloths, candles, and a romantic atmosphere. A favorable review by the Post and Courier brought them sudden renown and many diners, who become loyal customers.

In 1985 they moved to 235 King Street, and then in 1991 they opened a new space on 192 East Bay (now restaurant SNOB) where they stayed until 1994. Lucia still lives in Charleston with her current husband Bill. She is a supporter of Nuovo Cinema Italiano Film Festival and several charitable organizations.

Il Cortile del Re (1997-2015)

Massimiliano Sarrocchi, originally from Rome, and his American wife Erin Perkins opened the restaurant on 193 King Street when there was no authentic Italian dining spot in the heart of Downtown Charleston. The restaurant, with its charming courtyard, was composed of three former houses, built in the early 1800's. It became very popular at a time when the city was experiencing a growth in tourist visits, and it soon became an Italian landmark for the evenings in Charleston.

The owners' statement: "It is our intention to offer you our hospitality today and we wish tomorrow too. In our space we have made an "Enoteca con Cucina", which you can find in the big and small centers of Italy. A place for enjoyable conversations and traditional Italian foods. We offer big

WORLD WAR II TO THE LATE TWENTIETH CENTURY

and small plates as well as a full bar. .... We believe it is not necessary to spend excessively to enjoy quality wine. Please ask about wine specials as we are always tasting and experimenting with new options and vintages. We hope that you will enjoy the ambiance of our home....be it in our fireplace room, the front window, our beautiful courtyard.......we wish all to be healthy and happy and enjoy.

Our food is prepared at the moment for you ...your patience is our quality.

Buon appetito!

Grazie
Kim, owner"

167 King Street.

Pane e Vino (2008-2020)

Alfredo Temelini, from Treviglio (Bergamo), provided the inspiration for Pane e Vino, a typical Italian restaurant at 17 Warren Street. He arrived in Charleston in 2000 as an employee of an Italian furniture company. In 2001 he became the General manager at Peninsula Grill, and later went to work as a manager at Il Cortile del Re. When he took over Pane e Vino, he reformed it to suit his own dining tastes: "The menu was inspired by the cuisine of my native Lombardy, influenced by the cooking of my mother and grandmother from Pesaro. My grandfather was from Bologna, so my background was rich in menu ideas." The clients of Pane e Vino's were looking for an authentic Italian experience, and Alfredo still treasures "so many memories, so many friendships."

When asked which were the favorite dishes, promptly answers "The gnocchi e the pappardelle with duck sauce! I can proudly say that my clients were very demanding and challenging, I have never disappointed them. I never served spaghetti and meatballs or chicken with spaghetti. It would have been easy to bend to these American trends, but I resisted." No longer in the trade, during his restaurant career Alfredo was known for creating unforgettable parties, notably his Christmas Eve dinners.

Paolo Dalla Zorza brought Italian desserts to the South

Paolo's Gelato was an upper King Street staple for twenty years and was one of the pioneering businesses in that part of the city, along with Basil and Rue de Jean. Zorza is a native of Treviso and is a jack of all trades, with a background as a veterinarian, pilot, and gelato master. He moved to the American South to work as a pilot, but became intrigued by the lack of gelato offerings in the United States, so, he says, "I decided to fly back to Italy and start working for an Italian company that was making gelato. In the meantime, I started the preparations for my visa. I was lucky, because in 1998 it was easier for Europeans to come here. So I came back and I selected this place, which I found by chance and I thought it was perfect. There used to be an Italian ice shop here, and when I came, they told me: What, you want to open a gelateria?! With Italian ice we are already bankrupt, with gelato you will be super-bankrupt! And I told them: Please, give me a chance! And I've been here for 16 years."

His Charleston shop specialized in fruit flavored gelatos as well as egg and milk-based options, and in 2018 he remodeled and expanded his offerings to include pastas and Italian small plates, as well as wine and packaged Italian imported delicacies to go. He also imports thousands of gelato spoons, cups, and accessories though the port of Charleston each year for his shop and for resale. When asked what sets his gelato apart, Paolo noted the quality and authenticity of the ingredients for flavoring; "[other makers] buy a mix, they dump it in the milk or the water and they make it. So people see that I make the gelato from scratch and they like it, otherwise they would go and buy it from somebody else." Paolo has since closed his Charleston location and operates in Atlanta, Georgia.

CHAPTER 8:

SPOLETO FESTIVAL U.S.A.

While Charleston was known for its theatrical and musical prowess in the colonial era and had a run of fame with Dubose Heyward and Ira Gershwin's American opera *Porgy and Bess* in the 1930s, the city had largely lost much of its cultural momentum by the mid twentieth century. In the 1970s, the award-winning Italian composer and impresario Gian Carlo Menotti rectified that, with the help of Mayor Joseph P. Riley and College of Charleston president Theodore "Ted" Stern, by founding the Spoleto Festival USA in 1977, as an American counterpart of the annual festival in Spoleto, Italy (also founded by Menotti, in 1958.) Together the two festivals, which include a multitude of opera, dance, theatrical, and musical events in genres ranging from Classical to modern interpretive, comprise the Festival dei due Mondi. Menotti had struggled to find an appropriate counterpart city in the United States for the eponymous original festival, when he discovered Charleston: "I was about to lose all hope. Then a friend flew me down to Charleston and it was love at first sight. I made the marriage proposal on my first visit and the people of Charleston accepted immediately. It's intimate, so you can walk from one theatre to the next. It has Old World charm in architecture and gardens. Yet it's a community big enough to support the large number of visitors to the festival."

Joseph P. Riley Jr., Charleston's longest serving mayor (in office from 1975 to 2016), was kind enough to share his reflections on the origins of Spoleto. His words, written in January 2021, speak to the excitement of the early days of Spoleto U.S.A.'s inception:

"The creation of Spoleto Festival USA was one of the most important events in Charleston's history. It of course would have been impossible without the leadership and creative energy of Gian Carlo Menotti. It was a great honor and privilege to have the opportunity to work with Maestro Menotti in the creation of the festival. Gian Carlo often was quoted as saying that with Charleston it was love at first sight. Gian Carlo believed Charleston's beauty and antiquity made it the perfect backdrop for this world-class Festival of the arts. We were all most anxious about the beginning of the Spoleto Festival USA. The world's artistic leaders were quite taken with the idea of a relatively small American city providing a backdrop for one of the world's great arts festivals. The Festival's first year in 1977 was a smashing success. It exceeded everyone's greatest expectations, including those of Maestro Menotti and many of the great artists and performers who participated in the Festival. The Festival most positively shaped this city's history. Charleston accepted the responsibility of hosting a world-class arts festival and of maintaining this Spoleto's commitment to excellence in everything that we did. That first year, and for decades to follow, the excellence of the Festival and the beauty of Charleston have proven to be a perfect blend.   19 January 2021."

Charleston Magazine proudly reported on the inaugural festival in the 1970s that the Holy City had been chosen out of many American contenders even though it was small and with less theater space when compared to New York or Boston; "there are parallels between Spoleto and Charleston. Neither is large in extent or population. In terms of their countries' histories, both are ancient. For various reasons, both have escaped extensive modernization or even restoration- until recently. Both give the general impression of great age."

Menotti at a press release for the first Spoleto Festival, alongside Mayor Riley. Courtesy of Donatella Cappelletti.

In a recent article on the festival, the *Post and Courier* noted of the other founding participants: "There was Riley, the then-mayor of Charleston who courted the festival to Charleston and rallied the locals to embrace it, working every angle to ensure that it evolved into the much-lauded and well-oiled machine it has become. There was Ted Stern, the College of Charleston president who served on the festival's steering committee. He offered up campus facilities like Cistern Yard for performances and residence halls to house festival participants. There were other forces, too, radiating out from the festival with artistic endeavors that dovetailed with the main show, helping maintain the momentum of the heady festival days throughout the year." Menotti resided in the United States for part of his life but retained his Italian citizenship. He died in 1993 at age 95, although he had severed his ties with Charleston Spoleto by that point, due to personal conflicts and a clash of leadership with the managing director. The *New York Times* noted that although Menotti had "threatened for years, loudly and acrimoniously, to split with the American festival, and he finally did so in 1993, [he] will be honored in a free concert tomorrow morning, and he has figured prominently in conversation during the festival's early days."

Spoleto Festival remains one of the premier arts and musical festivals on the annual national calendar, with nearly half a million people visiting the two locations (Spoleto, Italy and Charleston.). The organizers and artistic directors behind Spoleto USA pride themselves on creating a unique and international assortment of productions each year, including featuring renowned Italian performers and pieces. The event became a major tourist draw in offering world class-performances normally only possible in large cities like New York or Boston for Charlestonians and visitors alike.

SPOLETO FESTIVAL U.S.A.

The grand George Street entrance of the newly renovated Gaillard Center.

Spoleto's Patroness: Countess Alicia Spaulding Paolozzi

Countess Alicia Spaulding Paolozzi (1918-2002) was born into a wealthy Boston banking family and was educated in private schools in the United States and Europe. She traveled abroad to Italy often, where she met and married Count Lorenzo Paolozzi, an artist and architect. The countess was a widely revered activist, businesswoman, occasional racecar driver, and a philanthropist. The newly married couple lived in Rome and Spoleto. Alicia met Gian Carlo Menotti in 1956 at a party when he was just beginning to look for a suitable US location for the American Spoleto Festival. She is credited with introducing him to Charleston, thus securing the city as the festival location. Ted Stern described her as "a remarkable woman, and the heart of the festival. We could always count on her for support." Paolozzi donated more than $500,000 to the festival during her lifetime.

The Countess had a plantation on Johns Island, a home on Kiawah Island, and a gallery and residence in the Fort Sumter House at 1 King Street for her frequent extended visits to Charleston. With her death in 2002, the *Post and Courier* ran a tribute to her that spoke to her many talents and generosity: "She was president laureate of the National Council of Women of the United States. She was a long-time officer and director of The International Council of Women, serving for many years as ICW liaison to the United Nations. She helped plan the U.N. Nairobi Conference. The Italian government recognized her for her generosity and support of the arts there. Paolozzi had a reputation for speaking diplomatically but frankly. If she helped a cause financially, she wanted to work for it, too. She was respected for her knowledge of world affairs, her business acumen and her insights into international relations. She also raced Porsches. David Rawle, who handled public relations for Spoleto Festival USA, said Alicia Paolozzi's fearlessness as a youthful racecar driver also marked her life view. 'She had an extraordinary vision and was fearless about getting involved in projects and enterprises way ahead of their time.'"

The Spaulding-Paolozzi Foundation has left a lasting impact on the Lowcountry even after the countess' death, providing large and generous donations toward environmental causes and sustainability, the South Carolina Aquarium, the International African American Museum, and to the Florence Crittendon Home. Dock Street Theatre, a beautiful historic venue for Spoleto and other cultural events, features a landscaped inner cortile that is named in honor of the Countess.

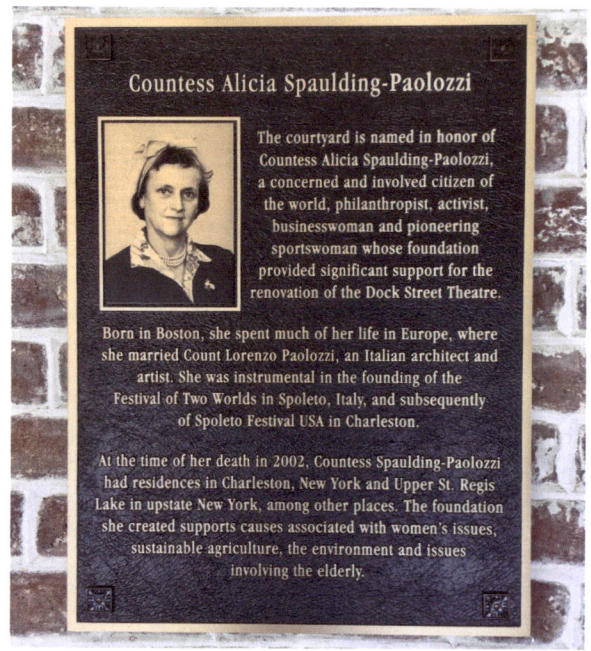

A plaque to Countess Alicia Spaulding Paolozzi in the courtyard dedicated to her at the Dock Street Theater.

SPOLETO FESTIVAL U.S.A.

"Italian by Adoption": Spoleto General Director Nigel Redden

Nigel Redden is the illustrious and much revered General Director of Spoleto Festival USA, a position he has held since 1986. Nigel's history with the festival, however, dates back to the late 1960s in Italy, where he was a student worker and volunteer for the original festival in Spoleto. He describes himself as "Italian by adoption," having moved there when he was 12. He went to high school in Italy and then to university in the US. His parents were still abroad, so he volunteered to work for the Spoleto Festival and returned to Italy for the following five years in the summers. Mr. Redden moved back to Italy in 1974 in Rome, then came back to the US in 1976. He joined Spoleto Festival USA in 1986 as the managing director.

When asked to compare the Italian festival and its US counterpart, Nigel noted structural and size differences, as Charleston is a bigger city than Spoleto; "The old part of the town [Spoleto] is quite small where the festival takes place, even more in walking distance than Charleston. It's a medieval town with Roman ruins scattered throughout. There's a difference from an audience point of view, because all of the venues are smaller with the exception of the final concert. For an American, there is a charm about Italy, its own special flavor. But the festival itself was much alike - chamber music defines the beginning of the festival day, which was brilliant there and here. There were different personalities, Charles Wadsworth was in the US and brought a real, personal charm. With all due respect to the old Gaillard, the Teatro Nuovo was much prettier; but the Dock Street beats the smaller Spoleto theaters and has better site lines than in the Caio Melisso. Spoleto couldn't possibly accommodate as many, 900 versus 2700 at peak in the old Gaillard, 200 in the Caio Melisso versus 463 in Dock Street. Tesso Romano could seat about 800 outside but is not the size of the Cistern Yard. However, the productions were equally entrancing. The festival in Charleston had a larger reach, and in addition there is the Piccolo Spoleto local performer festival. [In Spoleto] people from Rome would set up shops in the old medieval storefronts that had been turned into garages, so the city really came alive. When I came to Charleston, I had been very much in love with the festival in Italy, and then fell in love with the festival in Charleston more."

On the ratio of tourists and locals at the festivals, Nigel noted that a smaller group came from out of town to Spoleto compared to Charleston. When he was there in the 1960s, there were just a few hotels and poincianas. "Most people didn't stay in the small town overnight and most artists stayed with families in a room, which also happened in Charleston in the early years of the festival. Much of the audience came from Rome and drove in. The roads are now better so Florentians come too. There was an American contingent, wealthy Americans. Fred Koch, of the brothers, would come in for the festival."

When asked how the Charleston festival has grown and changed from its early founding in the late 1970s to the present, Nigel says, "the festival has evolved with the city in the sense that 'too poor to paint too proud to whitewash' still applied in the mid 80s. There were still shabby parts of the city and the theaters, Dock Street's roof leaked, and the plaster was coming off. And the Gaillard was hardly beautiful. Post Hurricane Hugo the city became far more polished, and it happened to the theaters and festival as well. In the early years it was high artistic standards but also a 'we can make it work' approach. Things have become more professional which has its pluses and minuses. It means it is more organized and less free form 'we can make do.' The quality of what's on stage has remained consistent, and the breadth, while the focus and content has changed to more contemporary, with the current directions in performing arts writ large. We've added more politically engaged works, such as a piece called Dead End Kids, which was very difficult and politically engaged. This content, as well as wonderful baroque mixed with more international works, more from Asia."

Spoleto Charleston does still have a sense of small-town closeness and local patronage, although reduced from the early days; "Mary Ramsey was wonderful, she was an institution. Early on she had people stay [for Spoleto], entertained regularly, and went to three or four parties a night, everyone invited her. That has changed, I'm not absolutely sure if it's because it's more expensive to put on parties. Chamber music has a group of patrons and friends, because they don't perform in evenings. The early 'hands-on' quality has gone away but it may well return. So many of the big houses have changed hands."

When asked for his fondest memories of the Spoleto USA festivals, Nigel shared, "my first memory of Charleston was as an audience member and I was invited to a dinner, all of a sudden someone said you should join us at SuSu Ravenel's house. I couldn't have been greeted more warmly, as a long-lost friend even though we hadn't met. I thought, if this is what Charleston is like I'd love to work here. There have been all kinds of special years, early on we did the *Marriage of Figaro* in the Dock Street, it was a luxury to do in a small theater. There was fussing over choosing a singer. Giancarlo directed and wanted to have the young-looking countess. We put together an extraordinary cast, Rene Fleming early in her career, and a generally young cast in their 20s early 30s. The young cast worked perfectly for the piece, as it became a coming of age and the sexual mores and find your place in the world". He also fondly remembers the 1991 *Places of the Past* and the *Peony Pavilion* Chinese performances, and *Porgy and Bess* at the Gaillard, and performances in the Memminger before it was renovated.

Nigel Redden plans to retire in 2021, making this his last Spoleto Festival as Director. Asked to reflect on the illustrious success of the Festival and to speak to the long-term cultural impact of the festival on the small city of Charleston, he answers: "in the long term, the Festival reminds Charleston of its heritage as a cultural leader in the past. Like Pachelbel here in the colonial era, and the early French language theaters. Charleston has a selective sense of memory, but it does remember. What Spoleto has done is remind us of that very distinguished part of its history. We also must remember that culture is about beauty to some degree, and Charleston is a place that is dedicated to that."

Art can be an important vehicle for promoting cultural diversity as well, and for bringing social issues to the forefront in constructive ways. To that end, Spoleto 2021 will host the world debut of *Omar*, an operatic piece. "I am Most eager for *Omar*, in 2021, it has enchanting music and is deeply moving. Omar was an educated man and had been a merchant in Africa and was Muslim. He was 37 when he was captured and was sold in Charleston in 1807 to a horrible local owner and fled to Fayetteville and was bought there. He wrote his bio in Arabic in 1830s and died enslaved in his 90s at 1863. Slavery is usually anonymous - this gives it a human face. His aria is extraordinarily moving. *Omar* will be the only one unmasked and often alone on stage." Comparing *Porgy and Bess* versus *Omar*, Nigel states, "not many American operas are written about specific places and what happened to communities. Writing about slavery in 2020 is very different than writing about a place like Catfish Row in 1920. Charleston has opportunities to create a dialogue around the Black Lives Matter movement and an unfair past. We can deal with it in a productive way, use art to meditate on it and highlight it." The world premiere of *Omar* seems a truly fitting finale for Redden's thirty-five years of creative genius with Spoleto USA.

A Spoleto Conductor Returns to Charleston: Lorenzo Muti

Conductor Lorenzo Muti was born in Spoleto Italy and fell in love with music at a young age, studying at the prestigious Curtis Institute and Julliard. He sang opera, made his debut as a conductor at the Spoleto Festival (Italy) and has since conducted across the world: with the London Symphony, Spoleto Festival, in Amsterdam, and throughout Italy. Muti taught opera and music history at Duke University and conducted the orchestra for College of Charleston. He has served as the Artistic Director and Conductor of the Chamber Orchestra of the Triangle (North Carolina) since 1988. He now lives in Charleston with his wife Jill Muti, an accomplished flutist who has performed in the Spoleto festivals in the US and Italy, and in Norway and Austria. She was chair of the Fine Arts Department at the Ravenscroft School in North Carolina in the 1990s and has been the Head of the prestigious Ashley Hall girls' school since 2004.

Lorenzo and Jill Muti with their son, Niccolo.
Photo by Heather Teets. Courtesy of Spoleto Study Abroad.

Lorenzo was kind enough to provide an interview about his early and continued involvement with Spoleto Festival and the arts in Charleston. He explained that he was invited as a young man to conduct at the first festival in 1977 and felt that it was an important chance to be part of the expansion of a cultural enterprise. He had lived in New York and Philadelphia while studying music but had never been so far South until the Spoleto invitation. He described Charleston as, "a real discovery, a new world, from a climate point of view, and the humidity! The city in 1977 was very different, a laid-back town, a lot of interesting buildings but they were falling apart and abandoned. A completely different landscape [from today.]"

In the early days of Spoleto, performers and artists stayed with local families, and Lorenzo lived with, "a really colorful family on Legare street and it was a great experience. This Allowed me to really get to know how Charleston worked and to meet a lot of people, it was a welcoming city. For a musician, the festival offered a top-notch orchestra, has always been a jewel of the organization. And the audience was wonderful and accepting." Similar to his hometown, Charleston was, "filled with energy, so artistic and colorful, and dedication on the part of the local people. I was here three weeks, and maybe ate at a restaurant twice, everyone whisked him from party to party, they were really excited. Like any other thing, it becomes more formal and structured. It loses some of the fresh quality and naivety."

Muti conducted several other concerts on return trips to Charleston and when his wife Jill was offered a position as the head of Ashley hall, she accepted because of Lorenzo's fond previous experience in the city. For them, "it is the closest in the US to being in a European town. We can walk and not need a car, which is unusual in American towns, and the architectural and artistic beauty." When asked what he misses about his hometown of Spoleto, Lorenzo reflected that is the surrounding region: "Charleston is beautiful but let's say, what will we do next weekend? Nature wise there is a lot, the beaches, plantations. But other centers that are attractive from a cultural point of view are further away. In Italy we can drive to a variety of cultural and gorgeous places at close disposal. People need beauty in life, to survive in such a tough world. Out the door, you're surrounded by beauty, a short distance from completely different and unique regions. Not even the food or wine, [but] the variety [or culture]."

Fortunately, the Mutis are able to return to Italy often and share the experience with others through their non-profit organization Spoleto Study Abroad, which they founded in 1997 to offer high school students and educators the opportunity to study in Italy. The mission statement is, "to enrich professional development opportunities for teachers, school administrators and interested adults through exposure to the historical, architectural, and cultural riches of the Italian arts and humanities with yearly tours to various regions in Italy." Each year since 1998 Spoleto Study Abroad has led four-week summer sessions abroad. Ashley Hall in its consortium of schools which recently bought a building to send detachments of students to Spoleto more frequently and for longer durations. When asked how they conceived of the education sponsorship component. Lorenzo replied, "[We have] always been in education, and arts. We've always believed in traveling, important especially when you're young, to explore and learn about the rest of the world. That's what I did, and I'm a product of this kind of cultural exchange. As well as the arts. We always tried to explore and make young people understand arts are not just individual compartments, the arts all have a strong influence on each other. Interaction of different artistic fields. Study abroad and in a situation where they can explore all the facets of a different artistic world. Spoleto the natural location, it's a fantastic place- really a perfect textbook. For over 20 years. We strongly believe in this and it's amazing the effect it has on the kids. A unique experience in their lifetime. Especially kids who have never been able to travel to a different place and environment."

Ansonborough had long been an enclave for Italian residents, and it was fitting that a new street running through a small planned urban development behind the Middleton Pinckney House on George Street (the Spoleto headquarters) was named Menotti Street, in honor of the Spoleto founder, who will forever be remembered in the city.

CHAPTER 9:

ITALIAN AMERICANS IN TWENTY FIRST CENTURY CHARLESTON

The Sottile Legacy Continues:

The Sottile brothers who arrived in Charleston from Sicily more than a century ago each experienced great success in their new city, and their descendants carry their legacy of business and community leadership and entrepreneur spirit. The children of the five Sottile brothers who remained in the United States, and of their sister Marie, became prominent Charlestonians and started their own families, marrying into prominent South Carolina families including the Longs, Ways, Altmans, Conlons, and Mannings, among others. The important lives and legacies of the families of each of the pioneering Sottiles warrants a book of its own; to name but a few of the many important Sottile descendants:

- Rosina Maria Sottile Kennerty (1898-1986, daughter of Nicholas Sottile) was the president of the Charleston Federation of Women's Clubs, and was a leader with the Girl Scouts, Red Cross, and Exchange Club. She authored *Plantations on the South Side of the Ashley River*.

- Santo Sottile Jr. (1903-1980) succeeded his father as president of Charleston Hotel and founded Heart of Charleston Motor Inn in the 1960s and was also a cattle farmer and real estate developer.

- Carmelina Sottile Thompson (1910-1991, daughter of Giovanni Sottile) worked as a secretary of Pastime Amusement Company and married Louis Franklin Thompson. They had one child, Carmela. Carmelina was the historian for the Sottile family, and compiled biographies of the Sottile Brothers, and acted as the genealogist of the family. She compiled two important books, *A Record of the Sottile Family* and *A Record of the Sottile, Millenium Edition,* for which the author of this book is immensely grateful.

Mary Ellen Long Way is the daughter of J.C. Long and Alberta Sottile Long, and the granddaughter of Albert Sottile of Pastime Amusement fame. She was interviewed by the College of Charleston for the *College Today* magazine when the Sottile Theater reopened after an extensive renovation to renew its Charleston Renaissance era splendor. She told the journalist that as a young girl about age five, she "remembers watching her grandfather depart on a chrome bicycle from his home- the yellow namesake Victorian house on campus- to wheel over to King Street. One by one, he would spot-check each venue. Mrs. Way and other family members were regulars at them, as each was given passes to attend all shows with a friend."

Mary Ellen married Charles S. Way in 1959 and the couple had three daughters, Alberta Freeman, Ellen Dudash, and Sally Wise Howle and two sons, Charles III and Leonard Darlington Way. Mr. Way is chairman of the board of the Beach Company, a position he has held for many years, and he has led the company to great success and expansion in the state. Knowitall.org, which conducted an interview with Mr. Way as part of a social studies curricular resource for South Carolina public schools, states, "Charles and Mary Ellen Way were recruited in the early 1980s to support the Spoleto Festival. In 1984, Way served as the organization's president, and from 1985 until 1991, he was chairman of the board. His fund-raising activities helped the foundering organization to become a major arts and tourism event for South Carolina. In 1991, he was named chairman emeritus. "Spoleto was just such a wonderful asset and a huge boon to the city of Charleston. It has brought a tremendous amount of money and attracted so many people to the city," Way said. And it has made an art lover of Charlie Way. "Spoleto offers such varied events, and I just like them all. I might not want to go to the opera four nights a week, but I do enjoy all the things Spoleto offers," he said."

Anne Darby Parker is the great granddaughter of Albert Sottile, and the granddaughter of Alberta Sottile Long (and the daughter of Joyce Long Darby.) Mrs. Parker is a renowned artist whose contemporary paintings hang in the best galleries of Charleston and beyond. She graciously provided an interview in September 2020, in which she discussed the legacy of the Sottile family, and how she as a fourth generation Italian American still feels a connection with the family's heritage.

Anne did not know "Papa" Albert Sottile, who died around the time she was born. When asked if her grandmother or other relatives spoke Italian at home, she said no; "My feeling is when he moved to America he wanted to acknowledge his culture but not his language as much. He didn't speak Italian at home and didn't teach his daughter. They were all devout Roman Catholics, though, and a lot of our traditions and holidays centered around that." Her mother was close with "Papa Sottile" and conveyed to her a strong sense of family values and entrepreneur spirit, "and [the brothers'] journey to reinvent themselves in America has permeated into our generation."

The Sottile experience was one of cultural blending in the true American "melting pot" sense. Albert married an Irish Catholic, who Anne knew and describes as more American or Anglo Irish in culture than her other relatives. "She didn't cook. She was kind but not musical or lively, although she was a community leader." Anne's mother, however, looks more Italian and plays the accordion, and the tambourine, "so at family events like weddings there is still a sense of celebration and [Italian] music and dancing." "My mom and aunt spent a lot of time with Papa Sottile, and even when I see family members today, I think, 'oh they really picked up the Italian, or the English/Irish, heritage' uniquely." The Italian celebratory nature was passed through the women in her family, as Albert only had one daughter, who in turn had daughters. Anne is one of five siblings, and one of her sisters in law is Greek; "she was born here of course but her grandmother never spoke English, only Greek, so her children and their children kept the ethnic traditions alive so intact."

Despite losing the Italian language, the Sottiles in Charleston today are still very interested in their Sicilian heritage. They have annual family reunions, and every five years they make a pilgrimage back to Gangi, Sicily. Anne notes, "it's fascinating to see the power of five brothers coming through Ellis Island. They were very successful. They came from a tiny city on top of a hill on a rural island. There's a power in being together and seeing the place. There are now hundreds of family members descended from the five brothers. [In Gangi] we got to meet Sottiles who live there and we have kept contact with them. They've also come here to America for one of the reunions! They speak no English and we don't speak Italian but everyone is warm and loving. I know they loved the climate here in Charleston because it's so similar to Sicily. You'll see really similar vegetation in Sicily. The [Sottile brothers] probably wanted to be somewhere that felt like home, a connection to the new place."

When asked why she thought Albert spoke so little Italian at home: "I don't know how much he felt, but I think they wanted to be American. They wanted to be modern, new, progress and entrepreneurial Americans. Otherwise, they'd probably have stayed in Italy. There was a reason for the move." Giovanni, the first brother to arrive, was one of the only to marry an Italian woman, giving him more opportunity or reason to speak at home. Albert Sottile held strongly to his Italian culture, however. The Sottile house on the College of Charleston campus that he built, "feels really Italian, in the design and craftsmanship. He had an interest in craft and his theaters reflect a European feel to me. He definitely brought in that flare. He wasn't a Shaker - he was more reflective of the old European influence from Sicily and you can see that in the architecture, and I think it has influenced our generation as well. I love marble, and music and art. [My Italian ancestry] has definitely shaped who I am but doesn't direct my day. We are still Roman Catholic, which nurtures and inspires me every day."

She also shared her favorite family stories that were passed down about Albert Sottile: "I feel like Papa Sottile brought the Old World to Charleston, as an entrepreneur, in a way that brought a more modern sense to the city - the theater and the cinema. I remember the fun stories about Clark Gable, and Liza Minelli, all the celebrities that came to the premieres here. He was a showman. He built the theaters, was a visionary contractor and builder, and had enthusiasm to bring art and entertainment to the people of Charleston. He brought a cross section of his potential and landed it here in King Street and in the Sottile house." As an artist and entrepreneur, Anne identifies with the Sottile spirit and appreciates the, "great spaces [Albert created] to come together to congregate and celebrate the arts. Who knows if that was part of the inspiration for later Spoleto? He came with no baggage - he didn't have to worry about a social clique like older Charlestonians. He was there for the American dream and decided on Charleston." And the people of the city are fortunate in his choice to settle here still today.

Nicholas C. "Nick Sottile" is the current historian for the Sottile family and the curator of the Sottile Family Reunion website, which includes a host of family photos and history, as well as images from the annual Sottile family reunions. Nick said that the highlight was the 2005 reunion, in which 72 South Carolina Sottiles "converged on the cousins in Sicily." Of the first Sottiles to emigrate to the United States, Nick aptly states, "they came with nothing to lose and created new successful lives. They were risk takers."

Richard Cox and the Spalviero Family:

Richard Cox is a third generation Italian American, born to Inez Spalviero Cox and Rutledge Eugene Cox Sr. Currently residing in Florida, his grandparents immigrated from Calabria to Chicago and then to Charleston, where Mr. Cox's parents, siblings, and himself grew up.

His grandparents, Albert E. Spalviero (1886-1950) and Maria Mormile Spalviero (1897-1975) immigrated to the United States separately. Albert went to Chicago to work in the railroad industry. Maria was in Calabria and they met through the post- she wrote letters to him for his mother and they struck up a relationship through writing. Albert eventually asked Maria to come to the states to marry him and she obliged, traveling to Ohio with her father to meet Albert in person at long last, and then going to Chicago together to wed. They came to Charleston in 1922 and Albert became a fruit and vegetable seller. Mr. Cox explained that Albert purchased goods coming into Charleston from the Sea Island truck farms and sold them from a cart around the city while living on Washington Street, where there was a small Italian district. Albert prospered and quickly transitioned to a brick-and-mortar store and had several locations in Charleston over the years: on Washington Street, Elizabeth Street at the corner of Ann Street, in Ansonborough near where the family lived, and then later on America Street after the family moved to Reid Street in the East Side (Albert is listed with his family at 45 Reid Street in the 1940 census as a vegetable vendor.) They then moved to the westside of the peninsula, purchasing a building at 192 Rutledge in 1944 and residing on Morris Street.

> **A. E. SPALVIERO**
> Cor. Ann and Elizabeth Sts.
> PHONE 9266
> —The—
> **Pennsylvania Meat Market**
> Is Now Open to Furnish You With the Best Meat at Exceptionally Low Prices—Eat More of It.

An advertisement for A. E. Spalviero from the *City Directory*.

Richard did not know his grandfather (who died in 1950) but was close with his grandmother Maria. When asked if she spoke Italian at home, Mr. Cox noted, "mother said Papa refused for grandmother to speak Italian, and to only speak English at home so the children would not have an accent. They would fight in Italian in front of the kids, but otherwise wouldn't speak it at home." However, she would meet and visit other Italian people in Charleston, and had Greek and Jewish friends, so as a child he was used to hearing accents and diversity. For Mr. Cox, Italian heritage shines through in foodways; "when I hear boiling water I think of my grandmother, she always had food cooking. My mother would give us meat or a full pasta dish to eat while she was cooking the actual dinner for later." He also carries on family traditions, such as placing flowers on loved ones' graves on holidays. His parents passed away recently, and he drove five hours to visit them on Christmas, as his grandmother had done for her lost family members.

Mr. Cox has traveled to Calabria to meet his family, and the resemblance was strong; they grabbed his nose and said, "oh, he looks just like his grandmother. They were reticent to show the original mountain house they lived in and were embarrassed about it, it's a little crumbly, centuries old. A Chicago relative who could speak Italian explained they weren't judging; they just wanted to see the roots, where they were from and then they were more receptive." Richard speaks fluent French and some Italian but the relatives didn't have much English; still, "everyone was laughing and having fun even though they couldn't always understand each other, the language barrier was not an issue," and they had the same food culture and love of conversation that Mr. Cox remembers of his grandmother. He describes the Italians he has met in his trips as "lovely and welcoming people."

CHAPTER 10:

ITALIANS IN CHARLESTON TODAY

Charleston continues to attract new residents from across the world who are allured here by the city's weather, surrounding natural beauty, culture, and the historic buildings. Many recently-arrived Italians note the city's Old-World character and the appealing combination of small town friendliness and city cosmopolitanism that many American's travel to Europe in search of. The city is indeed fortunate that Donatella Cappelletti, Giulio Della Porta, Mariano La Via, and several others have decided to share their talents and settle in the Lowcountry.

Professor Emeritus Mariano La Via

Among modern Charleston's longest-living Italian-born resident we find Mariano La Via, Professor Emeritus of the Medical University of South Carolina. Born in Rome in 1926, Mariano first came to Charleston in 1972 and settled here permanently in 1979. Dr. La Via is a specialist in immunology, specifically the field of Flow Cytometry and the role of stress in depressing the immune response. He was the first president of the International Clinical Cytometry Society., which supports researchers in current and emerging clinical applications of Cytometry throughout the world. A lover of the arts, he and his wife June are enthusiastic supporters of the Charleston Symphony Orchestra and the Nuovo Cinema Italiano Film Festival.

A Little History . . .

Mariano earned his MD Degree in Messina in 1949. In 1950 he was hired by the prestigious Istituto Superiore di Sanità in Rome; but he wanted to see what was happening outside Italy, particularly America. In 1952 he set sail for the United States. A professional connection led to the University of Chicago where he met Paul Roberts Cannon, President of the American Association of Immunologists. Chicago was a phenomenal experience for Mariano: here he worked among such luminaries as Enrico Fermi, winner of the Nobel Prize in Physics. Mariano felt that this was the place to be, the ideal place to pursue a career as Immunologist.

After a residency at the University of Chicago, Mariano moved on to teach in Denver and Atlanta. By 1979, he had authored two important books in Pathobiology and Immunology, and was invited to Charleston by Armand Glassman, distinguished professor of Immunology at the Medical University of South Carolina. Here Mariano La Via won important funding for his research laboratory in the field of cell analysis in the wake of the development of the Coulter Principle.

In late 1984, Dr. La Via initiated a series of conversations with other experts in the field concerning the possibility of organizing a conference on clinical applications of cytometry. Cytometry was growing as a diagnostic and monitoring technology in the clinical laboratory; the experts agreed on the need to establish a forum to exchange information, to present research data and to explore new clinical applications of the rapidly expanding technologies of image and flow Cytometry. This initiative led to the founding of the International Clinical Cytometry Society. This Society that has continued to grow, having been focused for years on discussions of flow cytometry and HIV infection. It was this work which enabled Mariano to meet and work with Anthony Fauci, Director of the National Institute of Allergy and Infectious Diseases since 1984.

Having retired in 2002, Mariano is now Professor Emeritus on the MUSC faculty, and he remains close to his former students. Mariano looks back fondly on his long relationship with the city Charleston. He notes, "Charleston was very different in the 1970s. I can say I saw it born. I cannot forget when Maestro Giancarlo Menotti came here with his idea of finding a "second world" for his "Festival di Spoleto" in Italy. I personally met him and I can confirm he was an incredible person. Absolutely charismatic, a genius. The Spoleto Festival was the engine of the Charleston Renaissance. Downtown was an unsafe wreck and with the birth of the Festival, our unforgettable Mayor Joe Riley managed to change the history of the city".

A supporter of Spoleto Festival USA since its founding, Professor LaVia says that since, "they had support from all over America, so I preferred to give some more to our dear Charleston Symphony Orchestra". Long time subscribers to the CSO, Mariano and his wife June also host musicians and chamber music concerts in their home. When the Italian cultural society Società Dante Alighieri established a Charleston branch in 2017, Mariano and June were among the first members.

Italian noble heritage: Donatella Cappelletti and Giulio Della Porta

Originally from the Umbria region of Italy, the Della Portas moved to Charleston in 2010. They had happened to end a 900-mile automobile vacation through the south in the Holy City and fell in love with it. As the Post and Courier noted in an interview in 2016, "They have become genuine ambassadors of the Italian arts in Charleston as well as sponsors and promoters of excellence in things Italian, from film to music to gardens and food. Much of the ambassadorship takes place in their historic home, now a classic blend of the best of Charleston and the best of Italy, filled with Italian art and statuary and marble."

The couple supports the Spoleto USA Festival and have often offered their home to host renowned after parties. They are also patrons of Charleston's Nuovo Cinema Italiano Film Festival, established in 2006. Donatella notes, "We have great affection for the Nuovo Cinema Italiano Film Festival. It's the only cultural event in South Carolina that focuses exclusively on Italian contemporary culture, with the bonus of opening the doors of America to young Italian talents – actors, animators and movie directors."

ITALIANS IN CHARLESTON TODAY

Giulio is a preservationist and designer who restored houses and buildings for more than twenty years on his ancestral property in the area of Gubbio. His family tree goes back to the age of the Italian Renaissance. Donatella explained that, "the title of Count was given to the Della Porta family in the year 1513 after their financial support to the Duke of Montefeltro's fight against the De Medici family. When the Duke won and kept the Duchy territory, he rewarded the Della Portas with the title and the land and two castles in Umbria (the countship). Since then, the Della Portas, originally from Modena, have always lived in Umbria."

Donatella was a newspaper journalist for 26 years prior to living in Charleston. Her love for architecture and art is a passion inherited from her father Roberto Cappelletti, preservationist when Heritage and Conservation were not yet popular themes. Giulio and Donatella worked together to open in Charleston a quintessential Italian boutique called The Hidden Countship in 2011. The shop's name is from the title of the book dedicated to the Della Porta family, the book which first brought them together. The store specializes in unique Italian handmade creations including jewelry, linens, porcelains and art.

When asked about how they conceived of the store and how they selected their one of a kind pieces, Donatella explained, "The project was to bring to the US artifacts coming from small but very high-end workshops of artisans and artists. It was amazing! We traveled for months through small villages to meet makers, who are now so proud to be selling their work in America."

Writer Robin Howard notes in Charleston Style and Design Magazine "Donatella and Giulio Della Porta say they instantly fell for Charleston,

Donatella Cappelletti and Giulio Della Porta at the Hidden Countship

and it's not a stretch to say that Charleston fell just as quickly for them. From the treasures shared through The Hidden Countship to the delightful and generous cultural exchanges, the Della Portas and Charleston, like Italy and America, will always be a good team."

Asked if there are any challenges to being Italian in the American South or if she gets homesick for Italy, Donatella said, "No challenges at all! The warmth of people did the magic. After the first year we had so many friends that we became addicted to our life in Charleston! It is really moving to meet so many people in love with Italy, who hold a lovely memory of an Italian trip or Italian friends. We heard enthusiastic stories from hundreds of people who have entered the store in the last 9 years. Oh, so many amazing stories! As a journalist, if I had kept better track of their names and stories I could write a book!"

War photo-reporter: Gian Luigi Scarfiotti

Gian Luigi Scarfiotti was born into a distinguished family in 1939 in Turin, Italy. His grandfather Lodovico Scarfiotti was one of the founders and the first President of FIAT, the Italian automobile manufacturer. His father was a German POW during World War II and later worked with a family cement company. His cousin Lodovico Scarfiotti Jr. won the Monza Gran prix, driving a Ferrari. Another cousin, Nando Scarfiotti, was a renowned theater and film scenographer, winning an Oscar for his work on Bertolucci's "The Last Emperor". Having studied Classics in Turin and Economy in Switzerland, Gian Luigi joined the family firm and developed a passion for photography, which became his life calling.

Based in Rome, Gian Luigi won photography assignments from such magazines as *L'Espresso*, *Paris Match*, *Newsweek*, the worked with publishers Rizzoli and Mondadori. His war reporting took him to Ireland, Northern Ireland, Lebanon and other Mideast countries. He finally settled in the Chianti region of Tuscany, where he became a commercial photographer. It was here that he met Terri, his future wife. A native Charlestonian, Terri knew Giancarlo Menotti, and was in Italy for Menotti's Festival dei Due Mondi.

Gian Luigi first came to Charleston with Terri in 1983. He arrived during preparations for the Spoleto Festival USA, and photographed rehearsals of Madama Butterfly at the Dock Street Theatre, as well as Mayor Joe Riley's welcome speech. He fell in love with Charleston's architecture, parks, and the surrounding rivers and marshes. The scenery afforded him unique photographic opportunities. In his own words: "Well, I'm back to the photography that has always been the focus point of my love for Charleston. The changeable weather offers me the unique opportunity to capture the magic moments with the colors of the clouds at the sunset, the movement of the waves or the wind bending the seagrass in the marshes... I was very lucky to be able to share my time between the "Holy City" and Tuscany, two extraordinary places of our world so different and so far from each other but both able to give me the wonderful gift of joy and serenity."

For the sake of Cinema: Professor Giovanna De Luca

Giovanna De Luca, Ph. D. is an associated professor of Italian at the College of Charleston. She was born and raised in San Giorgio a Cremano, Napoli and is well known in Charleston as the founder of Nuovo Cinema Italiano Film Festival (NCIFF). This is the only campus-based Italian film festival in the United States supported by the prestigious Istituto Luce in Roma. The success of the Festival, founded in 2006, has been achieved by a small volunteer team with a limited budget. The 13th annual NCIFF set an attendance record in 2019, every screening to capacity crowds, with nearly 3,000 attendees over the course of the four-day event.

The love for Cinema was instilled in Giovanna by her mother, who loved to watch Hollywood classics on the television. Giovanna's mother belonged to the generation that formed Italy's nascent middle class, a result of the post-World War II economic boom. Hers was an ambitious generation that prioritized education and the pursuit of professional careers. Giovanna's early years were informed by political unrest, mafia violence, political corruption in Naples and beyond and, not least, the great achievements of Diego Armando Maradona and the Naples football team. It was also a period rich in cultural productivity. She and her friends were found each Wednesday at the Naples Cinema Astra to watch art films.

After obtaining a Laurea in Foreign Languages and Literature (English and Spanish) at Suor Orsola Benincasa University in Naples, and teaching several years in the public school system, she married and moved to New York City. There, she earned her master's and Ph.D. in comparative literature with a specialization in Italian studies and Film studies at the City University of New York, under the guidance of Robert Dombroski and Andre Aciman, with essential support from Gaetana Marrone Puglia at Princeton University.

In 1999, she was awarded the Grand Marnier-Film Society of Lincoln Center Critical Essay Fellowship for her article on Francoise Truffaut's L'argent de poche, later published in Film Comment. This achievement further enhanced her enthusiasm for the study of cinema. For a decade, she taught courses at Lehman College, Hunter College, Princeton University and, ultimately, at Queens College as a visiting professor. In 2004, she took a tenure-track job at the College of Charleston.

She worked hard to expand the Italian Program, adding courses and shifting its emphasis so it might embrace a global vision and provide international opportunities to students. She started the NCIFF in 2006 and soon launched a successful study-abroad summer program based in Sorrento, Italy.

The NCIFF was Giovanna's response to a perceived void in Charleston, where local theaters rarely showed international films. The festival began with a retrospective of the works of Gianni Amelio. It developed into a significant four-day, red-carpet event drawing Italian filmmakers to Charleston and exposing students and local residents to a new world of creative production.

Nuovo Cinema Italiano Film Festival generally screens 13 films each year, typically at the Sottile Theatre, and welcomes directors, actors, screenwriters and others who discuss their work with audiences (and enjoy the offerings of our lovely city). A panel of expert jurors names the best film of the year, and a special trophy, made by Neapolitan artist Lello Esposito, is awarded. The festival, now the biggest of its kind on a college campus, has become quite well-known nationally and internationally. It receives support from Istituto Luce Cinecittà, MiBACT, Italian Cultural Institute of Washington D.C., South Carolina Humanities Council, and several local benefactors.

In 2014, Giovanna was named one of the city's 50 most influential people by Charleston Magazine. She was the recipient of the Trident Literacy Pat Gibson Founder's Award in 2019 and, later that same year, delivered a presentation at Charleston's Pecha Kutcha 35. Her academic writings have appeared in Filmcritica, Film Comment, Quaderni d'Italianistica, Forum Italicum, Italica, and Journal of Italian Cinema and Media Studies. She is the author of the book *Il punto di vista dell' infanzia nel cinema italiano e francese: rivisioni*. She is currently writing a book on the cinematic representations of the mafia, and co-authoring another volume about new Neapolitan cinema.

"Dreams are like stars": Enzo Caiazzo

Vincenzo (Enzo) Caiazzo, comes from Pomigliano d'Arco, a small town near Napoli in Southern Italy. He is the former Chairman of the Board of Global Aeronautica, a joint venture between the American company Vought and Alenia of Italy, formed for the assembly and the integration of large fuselage sections of the revolutionary Boeing 787 Dreamliner. He offered the following reminiscence:

"It was a beautiful sunny day in North Charleston on December 5, 2006 when I took the stage to deliver a speech for the grand opening of Global Aeronautica plant. At the end of my prepared speech, as I put the papers in the pocket of my jacket, I added an informal comment: 'A visit to Cape Canaveral has always been a dream of my generation. I was able to live this dream a few months ago and, when I was there, I was struck by a sentence written on a flag to commemorate a space mission: 'Dreams are like stars, you choose them as your guides and following them you reach your destiny'. Following our dreams, we have reached our destiny here in North Charleston.

Giovanna De Luca (left) on the stage of the Sottile Theatre in 2018 with Italian actress Sabrina Impacciatore. Courtesy of Donatella Cappelletti.

I have no doubt that an important part of the future of our companies and of our industry, now lies in South Carolina with the Global Aeronautica project that will be remembered as a pioneer in the aerospace arena."

Enzo was right. That day, the fate of the state changed dramatically, and South Carolina has become one of the most important centers in the world of the commercial aviation industry.

Enzo was the key player in the decision to bring the aviation industry in Charleston County, thus making a huge impact in the economic development of the State of South Carolina.

In December 2009 Boeing bought Global Aeronautica based on its strategic role in the 787 Dreamliner program. Later in the years, Boeing expanded the plant with a final assembly line, adding thousands of new jobs in the state. Finally, in October 2020, Boeing announced the move of all 787 Dreamliner production from Seattle to North Charleston. Today, the aerospace industry has evolved into a major pillar of the State's economy thanks to Enzo Caiazzo's initial commitment and decision in bringing the aviation industry in South Carolina.

On October 28, 2010, Mark Sanford, Governor of South Carolina, presented "The Order of the Palmetto", the State's highest civilian award for service, to Enzo in recognition and gratitude of his contribution to the economic development of the state. In his award letter, Sanford, praising Enzo, said, "Your work as Chairman of the Board of Global Aeronautica is paying rich dividends to our state in the form of jobs and in capital investments. The fact that our state has now emerged as a leader in the international aeronautics industry is in significant measure due to the

Aviation industry leader Enzo Caiazzo

confidence you placed in our workforce. For that, and for what you did in bringing Vought and Alenia together in South Carolina, we owe you a great debt of gratitude. The bottom line in all this is that Boeing would not be here if not for what you did. Congratulations - and thank you for all you've done for generations yet to come in South Carolina."

Enzo Caiazzo joined Aeritalia, the most important Italian aerospace company in 1978. Through the years, Enzo held a number of positions of increasing responsibility, residing abroad for extended periods, in the role of "global player" in the international aviation community.

Enzo earned a degree in Political Science from the University of Naples and has worked and lived in Italy, France, Australia, America. Among his executive positions: Vice President Marketing and Sales ATR, Head of Alenia Australasia, Senior Vice President Alenia Aeronautica Commercial Airplanes USA, Chief Operating Officer Alenia North America, Chairman of the Board Global Aeronautica.

On June 2, 2008, Enzo was awarded with the title of "Commendatore" (Knight Commander) of the Italian Order of Merit (Ordine al merito della Repubblica Italiana) for the international accomplishments in his career by decree of the President of Italian Republic Giorgio Napolitano.

Enzo has spent long periods of time in Charleston since he started visiting South Carolina in 2003 to follow the construction of the new plant of Global Aeronautica. Through the years, his love for the city and his connections with the community have never wavered, even when he lived and worked in other states or countries. Enzo now shares his time between Naples and Charleston, in his red-brick historic home in Ansonbourgh, riding his bike and walking along the charming streets of the old town.

Entrepreneur and Regina of Pizza: Laura Zanotti

Among the Charleston area's hundreds of restaurants only one is owned by a native Italian, Laura Zanotti. Laura came to the Lowcountry in 2007, when she opened La Pizzeria. It is the quintessential Italian restaurant, where the clients all seem to know Laura. "My place has become the hub of a sweet community; I love my customers and they love Italy. I feel blessed to be surrounded by so much kindness and thoughtfulness. La Pizzeria is a place for families, and I have seen so many children grow to adults and they still come to introduce their fiancé or tell me their College achievements."

Laura was born in Milan but moved as a young girl with her family to Abruzzo, where her Grandmother managed a hotel and restaurant business. She began her own career with a luxury giftware company in 1979, and she attended her first industry fair in New York City, exhibiting shaving brushes and giftware. Bloomingdales became a regular customer, and Laura dedicated herself to that calling until the recession of 1993. It was then that Laura decided to make a change and devote herself to the family trade.

She met Zaza Nakaidze, now her husband, in Boston, and they opened three restaurants together, including the Vecchia Roma. They then decided to leave the cold weather of Boston behind and toured the South, finally deciding to stay a while in Charleston. They stumbled upon an available restaurant space in a strip mall and decided to open La Pizzeria. They later expanded the offering to include a traditional trattoria menu, which was the key to their success. The restaurant is full most evenings, bustling under the supervision of Laura, Zaza, and the manager Eddie, who has become like a son to them.

"Our customers' favorite dishes are lasagna, eggplant rollatini, gnocchi Sorrento, and veal alla Laura. We source our produce, fish and meat locally, and import everything else from Italy. Most of all, I am very proud of offering healthy food. I cook only with the family olive oil, which I import after every harvest, and that makes the difference."

A tailored eye: Vittoria Garofalo

Vittoria Garofalo was born in Abruzzo, and has lived in Charleston since 1991. She was a third-generation tailor, having learned the trade in Italy from her father at a very young age. When she was 16, she was spotted by an aristocratic client of her father, who suggested Vittoria meet his American friend. That friend was a renowned wedding dress designer in Cleveland, Ohio, eager to hire a great seamstress like that young Italian girl. Vittoria would have loved to go but she was still young and the father simply said "no". Later, the designer came back to Abruzzo bringing 3 very special dresses to sew: "We worked day and night to make the American designer happy". Again the request to let Vittoria start a working life in America: "My father was not happy but his brother, the local priest, managed to convince him. It was an important move for me".

She finally arrived in Cleveland at the age of 19, not speaking English, and had a rude awakening. The designer, with the complicity of the cynical Italian aristocrat, expected her to work all day in the shop and the evening at home as a maid. This unhappy experience ended when she met Giovanni, an engineer from Modica, Sicily. After her father's initial rejection of a Sicilian suitor, Giovanni and Vittoria were finally married.

Laura with her husband Zara (left side) and the manager Eddie

Giovanni was a health technology engineer with Philips, and the company transferred him from Cleveland to work with MUSC. When Vittoria arrived, the wounds from hurricane Hugo were still visible and she remembers vividly the very first sight from the airplane: "It looked like someone had taken a saw and cut down all the trees, the city was suffering very much and so many houses were abandoned." Even in this condition, she could see the beauty of Charleston.

After her arrival Vittoria quickly gained the reputation as the best seamstress in downtown Charleston. She was noticed and hired by Saks Fifth Avenue, where she remained until the closure of the department store in 2011. She then was hired by the women's clothing store Rapport where she worked until 2017. Her work attracted clients from Charleston and distant states. Vittoria told the *Post and Courier* in 2011 that she vows to never let a customer walk out in an ill-fitting garment.

A painter from Sicily: Valentina Messina

Valentina Messina is an artist whose pieces are exhibited at the Charleston Artist Guild. She was born in Sicily, a land that is rich with the artistic heritage of the peoples who over the centuries colonized it, in that island of which Goethe said, "there is the key to everything". She grew up wandering among Phoenician ruins and Greek temples, Byzantine mosaics, amazing baroque virtuosity and the grace of Art Nouveau.

All these wonders had a deep impact on her soul. She started playing with brushes and pencils as a child but then, growing up, she had less and less time for creativity. Then one day she decided to quit her conventional job and start taking painting lessons. She also studied ceramics with the famous artist Susanna de Simone, learning from her all the origins and the legend from which inspire Sicilian ceramic objects.

She and her husband, Marco Madonia, were great admirers of America, never imagining that one day they would have called it their home. It happened a few months after their return from a trip on the east coast. They visited many historic towns, including Charleston. While Marco, who loves history, was captivated by sites and history of the Civil War, Valentina, as an artist, was fascinated by the inspiration of the lush gardens, the beautiful marshes and by the vibrancy of the artistic community. As Valentina liked to tell the customers of the ceramic shop she opened in downtown Charleston, after their last visit in the USA as tourists, they participated in the USA Green card lottery. To their amazement, they won! They took this as a propitious omen, said "Addio" to astonished friends and relatives and moved to Charleston with their daughter, Claretta.

They found everything they wanted; Valentina became an active member of the artistic community and later closed the ceramic store to focus on painting, gaining acceptance by local galleries. She and her family became citizens in 2018, fully embracing the values of the great Country that welcomed them so warmly.

Science against cancer: Alessandra Metelli

Alessandra Metelli, PhD, was born and raised in Spoleto, Italy. She works at the MUSC, currently investigating the role of monocytes and macrophages in Cancer Immunotherapy in the Carsten Krieg laboratory of Hollings Cancer Researcher. She graduated from the University of Perugia with a degree in Biology. While preparing her Master's in Biochemistry, she had the chance to meet a visiting professor from the far away Medical University of South Carolina. He was impressed by the skills of her and the group of 10 students focusing on Biochemistry and invited all of them to visit one day his laboratory at MUSC. At first no one followed up on the invitation. But, just a year later, in 2009, Alessandra's fiancé Andrea Muti received an invitation from Ashley Hall School in Charleston, to teach Italian Language and History. So Alessandra accepted the invitation to visit MUSC and she landed in Charleston in 2010. It was meant to be.

She was immediately accepted as a visiting student and then she was advised to apply for a PhD in Immunology. "So, five years of hard work began, it was tough but exciting. I was enthusiastic for the amazing opportunity, for the incredible environment with people literally from all over the world and so highly qualified. I felt honored to work with Dr. Zihai Li". She focused on the field of Cancer Immunology with Doctor Li and then she started a brilliant career filled with publications, awards, international meetings. She fell in love with Charleston, which became her home, the place where she married Andrea and where their first son Matteo was born.

Alessandra also found a passion for teaching, first as a graduate student, and later mentoring new students in the laboratory. She has also volunteered to teach high school students to engage them with biology, human immunology and environmental science.

"This is truly a beautiful city to live in, we love and appreciate so much the warmth of people. We are amazed by the thoughtfulness of Charlestonians. When our baby was born, we had every day, for one month, our friends and colleagues bringing dinner to us. We couldn't believe it! Later I found out they had filled a spreadsheet to organize shifts to help us! We couldn't hope for a better community."

Metelli with her husband husband Andrea and her son Matteo

Italians and Italian-American Shipping to the Southeast, By the Numbers

The Consulate General of Italy for the Southeastern region is currently located in Miami, Florida. Their purview includes South Carolina, Georgia, Alabama, Florida, Mississippi, Puerto Rico, and the small islands off the coast that are US territories, including the Bahamas. Their office notes that there are 44,354 Italians in their region, 1,041 of which are residing in South Carolina. There are currently 35 Italian firms operating in the state.

Shipping between the southeastern United States and Italy has increased steadily in the last decade, with over $5,770,600,000 in Italian exports coming in 2018 alone. Of this, 6% was wine, 26% was machinery, 14% was eyeglasses and frames, and 10% was vehicles. A large portion of these Italian goods and commodities arrive to South Carolina, to the Wando-Walsh Terminal in Mount Pleasant, which is operated by the Mediterranean Shipping Company.

Mediterranean Shipping Company (MSC)

MSC Mediterranean Shipping Company (MSC) is a global business engaged in the shipping and logistics sector. Present in 155 countries, MSC facilitates international trade between the world's major economies and among emerging markets across all continents.

Founded in 1970 and headquartered in Geneva, Switzerland, since 1978, MSC is a privately-owned organisation. A world leader in container shipping, MSC has evolved from a one vessel operation into a globally-respected business with a fleet of 570 vessels and 100,000 staff.

The company delivers goods and services to local communities, customers and international business partners, calling at 500 ports on 215 trade routes and carrying some 21.5 million TEU (twenty-foot equivalent units) annually via a modern fleet, equipped with the latest green technologies. With access to an integrated global network of road, rail and sea transport resources, MSC prides itself on delivering global service with local knowledge.

Over the years, MSC has diversified its activities to include overland transportation, logistics and a growing portfolio of port terminal investments. Today, the company's focus remains true to its roots, as it continues to build and retain long-term trusted partnerships with customers of all size and scale.

ITALIANS IN CHARLESTON TODAY

MSC USA opened in 1985, serving the American market for over 35 years. In the country, the company stands for 1,100 employees, 9 offices, 20 ports, 36 weekly services, 75 inland ramps and over 5.3 million TEU moved per year. The MSC Charleston office has become the largest branch office in the USA, employing 392 people of which 15% originally from Italy. The first MSC office in Charleston was opened in 1993. Since 2008, the company has been located on Watermark Boulevard, Mount Pleasant.

The Dante Alighieri Society, Charleston Chapter

Besides several unique and culturally important Italian-owned businesses, Charleston is also fortunate to have one of only nine chapters of the Dante Alighieri Society in the United States. The Society was founded in 1889 to celebrate Italian language, culture, and arts, and to unite all persons interested in Italian heritage, both native and foreign born. The Society meets on the second floor of the Hidden Countship for its regular meetings. The inaugural ceremony for the Charleston Chapter was attended by consul to Italy for the southeastern US, Dottoressa Gloria Marina Bellelli; director of Dante Alighieri, Miami Chapter, Claudio Pastor; and Naples sculptor and painter Ferdinando Ambrosino. The Society seeks to foster connections and advance knowledge of the myriad ways that Italians and Italian Americans have impacted and improved the communities in which they live and travel; in fact this book, which was commissioned by the Society, is just a small way to celebrate the deep and lasting contributions of Italians in Charleston, South Carolina, in a mutually beneficial relationship that will continue for decades to come.

CONCLUSION

Charleston is a beautiful and important historic city that was shaped by various diverse residents past and present, including a cadre of Italians who have worked to enhance our community in myriad ways. With a rich history dating to the colonial era, the city is home to the oldest Italian and Italian-American community in the southeast. Some immigrants worked as laborers and farmers and persevered in the face of language barriers and prejudice. Other early Italians like the Chiccos, Sottiles, and countless others in the late nineteenth century arrived with little and became successful merchants, business owners, restaurateurs, real estate developers, and politicians. From the colonial era to the present, they have enhanced the city's artistic and cultural life. Part of the city's tourism success is owed to the world-renowned Spoleto Festival USA, conceptualized, performed by, and patronized by Italians. Newly arrived Italians and the Italian American descendants of earlier immigrants will doubtless add to the city's vibrancy, diversity, and cultural life for centuries to come.

BIBLIOGRAPHY

Angeloni, Gabriella. *Reading Material: Personal Libraries and the Cultivation Of Identity In Revolutionary South Carolina.* (Doctoral dissertation, University of South Carolina, 2018.

Bass, Jack and W. Scott Poole. *Palmetto State: The Makings of Modern South Carolina.* Columbia: University of South Carolina Press, 2009.

Berg, Dave. "World War Two Prisoners of War in Charleston." https://www.ausa.org/coastal-south-carolina-chapter/blog/world-war-ii-prisoners-war-charleston (accessed 15 May 2020.)

Autobiographical essays generously provided by:
- Dr. Mariano La Via
- Dr. Giovanna De Luca
- Alessandra Metelli
- Valentina Messina
- Donatella Cappelletti and Giulio Della Porta
- Gian Luigi Scarfiotti
- Laura Zanotti
- Enzo Caiazzo

Butler, Nicholas Michael. *Votaries of Apollo: The St. Cecilia Society and the Patronage of Concert Music in Charleston, South Carolina, 1766–1820.* Columbia: University of South Carolina Press, 2007.

Butler, Nicholas Michael. "The Myth of the Holy City." https://www.ccpl.org/charleston-time-machine/myth-holy-city (accessed 3 March 2020.)

Charleston City Directories. 1803- present. Various printers

Charleston County Deed Books, 1700s- present. Held at the Charleston County Register of Deeds (formerly Register of Mesne Conveyance.)

Charleston City Paper. "Just shy of celebrating 20 years, Paolo's Gelato is among those that needs help to survive the coronavirus." 10 April 2020.

Charleston Evening Post. Microfilm, South Carolina Room, Charleston County Public Library.

Charleston Magazine. "Ciao Bella! A pair of Italian immigrants fall hard for an historic Ansonborough single." January 2014.

Charleston Magazine. "Roman Remains: John Izard Middleton's Visual Souvenirs, 1820-1823." February 2010. https://charlestonmag.com/features/drawn_to_the_classics (accessed 6 December 2020).

Charleston Magazine. "The Arts: Spoleto, '77." September 1976, pg. 8-10.

Charleston Style and Design. "A Charleston house gets an Italian-style makeover." Robin Howard. https://www.charlestonstyleanddesign.com/blog/noble-transformation/

City of Charleston. *Charleston City Yearbook, 1928.* Charleston: Walker, Evans, and Cogswell, 1929.

College of Charleston. *The College Today.* "Albert Sottile Had a Real Sense of Theater." 2 July 2019.

Consulate General of Italy, Miami. Brochure for Southeastern Region, produced 2019.

Coulter, E. Merton. "A List of the First Shipload of Georgia Settlers." *Georgia Historical Quarterly,* Vol. 31, No. 4 (December 1947), 282-288.

Daniel, Pete. *The Shadow of Slavery: Peonage in the South, 1901-1969.* Chicago: University of Illinois Press, 1990.

Dawson and DeSaussure. *Census of the City of Charleston, for the Year 1848.*

Della Porta, Giulio. *The Hidden Countship.* Petruzzi Editore, 2001.

Findagrave.com. Accessed March and April 2020.

Ford, Frederick A. *Census of the City of Charleston, South Carolina, for the year 1861.* Charleston: Ryans and Cogswell, 1861.

Gable, Carl. "The Path from Villa Cornaro to Drayton Hall." https://www.draytonhall.org/the-path-from-villa-cornaro-to-drayton-hall-by-carl-i-gable/ (accessed 1 December 2020).

Gleeson, David. "Immigration." *South Carolina Encyclopedia.* https://www.scencyclopedia.org/sce/entries/immigration/ (accessed 16 May 2020.)

Hammond, John. "Nazi Troopers in South Carolina, 1944-1946." *South Carolina Historical Magazine,* Vol. 81, no. 4 (October 1980), 306-315.

Hidden Countship, "Our Story." https://www.thehiddencountship.com/pages/our-story

Historic Charleston Foundation. Historic photo and postcard collections- La Brasca's; 105 East Bay Street; St. Mary's Catholic; 158 Church Street.

Howard, Robin. "The Italian Connection: the Hidden Countship celebrates five years in Charleston." *Charleston Style and Design.* https://www.charlestonstyleanddesign.com/blog/the-italian-connection/.

Interviews generously provided by:
- Parker, Anne Darby. Conducted by Christina R. Butler, 22 September 2020, 9:30 am, via telephone.
- Cox, Richard. Conducted by Christina R. Butler, 4 January 2021, 9:30 am, via telephone.
- Redden, Nigel. Conducted by Christina R. Butler, 4 January 2021, 2:00 pm, via telephone.
- Sottile, Nicholas C "Nick". Conducted by Christina R. Butler, 7 January 2021, 2:00 pm, via telephone.
- Muti, Lorenzo. Conducted by Christina R. Butler, 6 October 2020, 9:30 am, via telephone.
- Riley, Joseph P. Jr. Via email, January 2021.

Iorizzo, Luciano J. *Italian immigration and the impact of the padrone system*. New York: Arno, 1980.

Janneh, Alhaji. "Thrombin contributes to cancer growth by overpowering the immune system." *MUSC News*. https://web.musc.edu/about/news-center/2020/03/04/thrombin-and-cancer-growth (accessed 4 December 2020).

Knowitall.org. "Charles S. Way Jr." https://www.knowitall.org/video/charles-s-way-legacy-leadership-profile

Lancaster, Clay. "Italianism in American Architecture before 1860." *American Quarterly,* Vol. 4, No. 2 (Summer 1952), 127-148.

Laravista. "Paolo Dall Zorza: they call me the Cartier of gelato!". 24 October 2015.

"Lorenzo Muti." https://www.chamberorchestraofthetriangle.org/conductors (Accessed October 2020.)

Madden, Richard C. *Catholics in South Carolina: A Record*. Maryland: University Press of America, 1985.

Marsh, Ben. *Unraveled Dreams: Silk and the Atlantic World, 1500–1840* (New York: Cambridge University Press, 2020), 271–78, 298.

Marsh, Ben. "Silk Hopes in Colonial South Carolina." *The Journal of Southern History.* Vol. 78, No. 4 (November 2012), 807-854.

Mazzulli, Theresa. "Where Did Trajetta Go?" *Boston Intelligencer.* 20 March 2012.

McDaniel, George. "Drayton Hall." *South Carolina Encyclopedia*. https://www.scencyclopedia.org/sce/entries/drayton-hall/

McInnis, Maurie D. *The Politics of Taste in Antebellum Charleston*. Chapel Hill: University of North Carolina Press, 2005.

McInnis, Maurie D. *In Pursuit of Refinement: Charlestonians Abroad, 1740-1860.* Columbia: University of South Carolina Press, 1999.

Miller, Randall M. "Catholics." *South Carolina Encyclopedia. https://www.scencyclopedia.org/sce/entries/catholics/* (accessed 15 May 2020.)

Mrs. Astor and the Gilded Age. "Huntington Hartford." https://mrsastor.com/content/10/ (accessed 18 September 2020.)

Motes, Margaret Peckham. *Migration to South Carolina*. Clearfield Company, 2005.

News and Courier. "Countess Paolozzi Confident Spoleto Will Be Successful." 7 November 1976.

News and Courier. "How it Began: Countess recalls genesis of Spoleto." 7 June 1986.

News and Courier. "Duke says Italian service units doing valuable work." 20 August 1944.

New York Times. "Spoleto Festival USA: An Italian Ghost in Charleston." 30 May 1997.

New York Times. "Mrs. Hartford A Prince's Bride' member of society in New York and Newport wed to Prince Guido Pignatelli." 26 April 1937.

Poston, *Buildings of Charleston*. Columbia: University of South Carolina Press, 1996.

Post and Courier. "Women's clothier Rapport, makeup boutique CosBar stepped up when Saks left King Street." 2 March 2011.

Post and Courier. "The harmonic convergence that made Charleston a music town." 8 August 2020.

Post and Courier. "Spoleto's Paolozzi Dies." 16 April 2002.

Post and Courier. "Ambassadors for Italy." 2 November 2016.

Preservation Consultants, Inc. *Sullivan's Island Historical and Architectural Survey*. Charleston: Preservation Consultants, 1987.

Richardson, E.P. "Allen Smith, Collector and Benefactor." *American Art Journal*, Vol. 1, No. 2 (Autumn 1969), 5-19.

Sass, Herbert Ravenel. *Stories of the South Carolina Lowcountry, Vol. III*. Michigan: J.F. Hyer, 1956.

SCETV. "The Case of Giovanni Sanguinetti." https://digital.scetv.org/teachingAmerhistory/lessons/HistoryMysteryTheCaseofGiovanniBaptistaSanguinetti.html (accessed 16 May 2020.)

Scott, K. *Rivington's New York Newspaper: Excerpts from a Loyalist Press, 1773–1783*. New York, 1973.

Shick, Tom W. and Don H. Doyle. "The South Carolina Phosphate Boom and the Stillbirth of the New South, 18667-1920." *South Carolina Historical Magazine*, Vol. 86, No. 1 (Jan. 1985), 1-12, 14-15, 17-31.

Smith, Henry Augustus Middleton Smith. *Historical Writings of Henry A.M. Smith, Vol. 1-3*. Spartanburg, South Carolina: Reprint Company, 1988.

Smith, Patricia Lowe. *Volumes that Speak: the Architectural Books of the Drayton Library Catalog and the Design of Drayton Hall*. Clemson Master's Thesis. May 2010.

Smith, Shelley E. "Architectural Design and Building Construction in the Provincial Setting: the case of the colonial South Carolina plantation house." *South Carolina Historical Magazine*, Vol. 116, No. 1 (2015), 4-28.

Smyth, William. *A Southern Odyssey: South Carolinians Abroad in the 1850s.* Master's Thesis, University of South Carolina, 1977.

Spartanburg Herald. "World renowned artists to gather in Charleston." 26 March 1976.

Snowden, Yates. *History of South Carolina, Vol. III.* Chicago: Lewis and Company, 1920.

Sottile, Nicholas C. *Sottile Family Reunion.* http://www.sottile.org/ "Sottile Family, 1889-2008." Accessed 17 May 2020.

South Carolina Historical Society, biographical vertical files. 30-4 Sottile.

Spoleto Study Abroad. "About Us." https://spoletostudyabroad.org/who-we-are (Accessed October 2020.)

Thompson, Carmelina Sottile. *A Record of the Sottile Family of Charleston, South Carolina.* Self-published, 1983. Held by SCHS.

United States Census records, South Carolina, 1790-1940.

Vertical Files: Sottile, Chicco, Italians in Charleston. South Carolina Room, CCPL.

Vincent Chicco's. "About." https://www.holycityhospitality.com/vincent-chiccos/ (accessed 18 September 2020.)

Underwood, James. Ed. *The Dawn of Religious Freedom in South Carolina* (Columbia: University of South Carolina Press, 2006.

APPENDIX 1: TRANSCRIPTION FROM MOTES, MARGARET PECKHAM. MIGRATION TO SOUTH CAROLINA- 1850 CENSUS.

Born in Italy:

Angelo, James. 35, fruiterer. Charleston

Annlino, Leonardo, 28, seaman. Charleston. On southern ship Southerner

Antony, William, 37 mariner

Augustine, Nicholas. 27, Statuary moulder.

Barranel, Antonio, 23, mariner (household of Augustine)

Bonneface, Lewis, 32, rigger

Bosson, Francis, 44m fruiterer

Broudine, Augustine, 16, fruiterer

Burrow, Emile, 28, fruiterer

Cameale, Angelo, 34, fruiterer

Costellen, Joseph, 35, fisherman

Currier, C, 38, fruiterer

Decosta, JF, 48, musician

Drago, Andrew, 26, merchant

Drago, Antonio, 25, merchant

Drago, Blanko, 58, female

Drago, Caroline, 16 female

Drago, Olivia, 18 female

Forre, A Della, 70, saw mill

Frances, John, 44 fisherman

Gambale, A, 39, merchant

Gastey, Arnise, 38 laborer, in poor house

Jacob, Mathew, 55 shopkeeper. In hose of Nicholas Talerand (53, Italy)

Jacob, Peter, 19, clerk. Same as above

Josephs, SJ, 22 mariner

Judas, Charles, 40, cutler. Prisoner

Judgee, Charles, 39, cutler

Lenar, Joseph, 32 clerk

Lewis, P, 23, shopkeeper

May, Mary 34 female (in house with John May of Rhode Island)

McHugh, Petronella, 25 female (in house of Mary McHugh of Ireland)

Monteveda, Geavana, 20, seaman

Moroso, Anthony, 30, fruiterer

Morrello, Jane, 45 female (in house with N Morrello of Gibraltar)

Musso, A, 30 fruiterer

Natael, P, 40 tavern keeper

Padron, Ferdenand, 42 rigger

Palmeda, Charles, 30 physician

Pattena, Joseph, 41 fruiterer

Pergen, L 25 shopkeeper

Petah, Joseph, 31 shopkeeper

Petah, Maria, 25 female

Peters, Carolina 32 female

Rasnel, Antonio, 33 laborer

Rasnel, Joana, 19 female

Salvo, Corado, 63 clerk

Salvo, J 48 painter

Slavick, JL, 27 rigger

Tallerand, Nicholas 53 clerk

Vadet, Joseph, 25 mariner

Whyte, Joseph 70 confectioner

Williams Joseph, 32 mariner

www.ingramcontent.com/pod-product-compliance
Lightning Source LLC
Chambersburg PA
CBHW040238170426
42811CB00127B/1810